# RIDING THE NORTHERN RANGE

## Poems from the Last Best-West

## Edited by Ted Stone

## WRITING WEST

**Red Deer College Press**

THE PUBLISHERS Red Deer College Press 56 Avenue & 32 Street Box 5005 Red Deer Alberta Canada T4N 5H5. Cover Art and Design by Kurt Hafso. Text Design by Kurt Hafso and Dennis Johnson. Printed & Bound in Canada by Parkland Colour Press for Red Deer College Press.

ACKNOWLEDGEMENTS The publishers gratefully acknowledge the financial contribution of the Alberta Foundation for the Arts, Alberta Culture and Multiculturalism, the Canada Council, the Federal Department of Communications and Red Deer College. Special thanks to Patricia Roy and Susan Toy for their assistance in the preparation of this book.

The editor gratefully acknowledges the many people who helped with this collection. Special thanks to Coralie Adams of the Alberta Cowboy Poetry Association, Cyndi Smith of Coyote Books, Doris Bircham, Katie Kidwell, and Gwen Petersen for their help in finding poems or contacting poets. Thanks to Jim Green and Dennis Johnson for their advice and enthusiasm, and thanks to the staffs of the State Historical Library in Helena, Montana, and the Glenbow Archives in Calgary, Alberta, for their assistance in finding poems from the early years of the Northern Range. Thanks to Coteau Books for permission to reprint poems from *Grasslands* by Thelma Poirier. Thanks also to Slick Fork Music for permission to use the lyrics of Ian Tyson's song "Springtime."

CANADIAN CATALOGUING IN PUBLICATION DATA
Main entry under title: Riding the Northern Range
(Writing West)
ISBN 0-88995-100-4
1. Cowboys–Poetry. 2. Cowboys' writings, Canadian (English)–Canada, Western.* 3. Cowboys' writings, American–West (U.S.) 4. Canadian poetry (English)–Canada, Western.* 5. American poetry–West (U.S.) 6. Canadian poetry (English)–20th century.* 7. American poetry–20th century. 8. Canada, Western–Poetry. 9. West (U.S.)–Poetry.
I. Stone, Ted, 1947–   II. Series   PS8283.C6R5   1993   C811'.5408'0352636
C92-091841-7 PR9195.35.C69R5   1993

# CONTENTS

# INTRODUCTION

*Riding the Northern Range* is a fitting title for this book. It has come about after years of riding back and forth across the region, in cars and pickup trucks, collecting and writing stories. Sometimes the stories have been called journalism, sometimes fiction, history, or folklore. Often, it seems as if the riding has made as big an impression on me as the stories.

The Northern Range (in my definition, roughly Montana, the Dakotas, the Canadian prairies, and parts of British Columbia) is a land of open spaces and surprising vistas. I'm continually awed by the dominating presence of the landscape. It's a landscape of sky as much as earth, often beautiful, but underscored with a lurking ferociousness always as close as the next cold front, blizzard, heat wave, drought, thunder, or hail storm.

Maybe that's why I admire the people of the region so much. The Northern Range is tough, unforgiving country, and it seems to have bred a persistent toughness and self-reliance into its citizens. The Northern Range is a land of extremes—extreme heat in summer, extreme cold in winter. People say the wind can blow your soul away.

At times, the Northern Range can be so dry crops refuse to grow and the grass withers and dies. Then, when rain finally comes, it often comes so fast and fulsome that most of it runs off into flood-swollen creeks and rivers instead of soaking into the drought-hardened ground. This is not a place for the weak-willed. Pioneers in other regions of North America faced hardships, but few places furnished them so abundantly as the Northern Range.

The Northern Range was North America's last old-West. It was the end of the trail for the great cattle drives of the 19th century. It was the last place where grass was free for the grazing. When politics, homesteaders, barbed wire, and weather finally conspired to end forever the open cattle-ranges—and Charley Russell had moved into Great Falls to paint the life he'd lived and observed—the days of the old-time cowboy were mostly over.

But the influence of those early years persists. The culture of the cattle industry came early and stayed. Ironically, in many areas, there are more cattle today than there were during the heyday of the open range. The ranches are smaller now, but there are more of them, and livestock production is still an important part of the entire region's economy.

The cattle culture moved north out of Texas in the years immediately following the Civil War. As the great prairie grasslands were emptied of buffalo and the aboriginal peoples starved into submission, new land opened for grazing. Texas had huge herds of semi-wild cattle and, as railroads penetrated the West—giving access to eastern markets—the southern cattle were brought north in increasing numbers to stock the new grazing lands.

The roots of North American cattle culture reach farther south than Texas. They start with the Mexican *vaqueros*, who taught American cowboys how to handle the wild, long-horned cattle of Mexico and south Texas. The lessons of the *vaqueros* spread as the great herds moved north. The language of contemporary ranch people, even those as far north as the Peace River country of Alberta and British Columbia, is laced with words that come, often in somewhat mangled form, from those first Spanish-speaking cowboys.

Today, cowboys dally up, a phrase created from the Spanish *da la vuelta* ("to take a turn"), by wrapping their lariat (from the Spanish *la reata*) around their saddle horn after lassooing *(lazo)* a bronco ("rough or unruly"). They still go to rodeos (from the Spanish for rounding up cattle into a ring). The word ranch itself is from *rancho*. Stampede is from *estampeda*. Even the original cowboy, the *vaquero*, was Anglicized and made a buckaroo.

But on the Northern Range, cattle, like the society and culture that developed around them, didn't come into the territory solely from the south. Cattle also came into the region from the east and even the north. The first bulls to arrive at the North West Cattle Company's Bar U Ranch in

Alberta were eastern bulls bought at the Chicago stockyards.

Small bands of cattle were brought up the Missouri River into Montana from the eastern United States long before the big herds arrived from the south. The first cattle turned out to pasture in southern Alberta were in a small herd John McDougall bought from the Hudson's Bay Company at Fort Edmonton in 1871. Indeed, the first cattle brought to the Northern Range came to Manitoba from Europe, via Hudson's Bay, before 1815.

Manitoba was also the setting for one of the earliest and most well-known cowboy songs to come out of the Northern Range. The song "Red River Valley" was written shortly after the Red River Rebellion in 1870. It wasn't thought of as a cowboy song at first; it was about a Metis woman who fled to Montana in the aftermath of the rebellion. Within a few years, however, the song was being sung, with additional lyrics, throughout the Northern Range. Probably, most of those who sang it mistakenly assumed the lyrics referred to the Red River of the South, a place most Texas cowboys who trailed cattle north knew more about than Manitoba's Red River.

In the early days of the Northern Range, cowboys sang and recited popular songs, folk ballads, and well-known poems from all over. Often the original verse was adapted to suit local conditions, experiences, and sensibilities. Indigenous verse came gradually. Many early cowboys harbored a strong strain of anti-intellectualism, so writing poetry was not always a socially acceptable form of activity.

But poetry had a more widespread following in the 19th century than today, among people of the West as well as other regions. As the country was settled, a few cowboys and ranchers began to write their own poems to reflect their life and times. Poetry was memorized and recited, sometimes by its authors, sometimes by others. By the turn of the century, chapbooks of Western verse were being published all across the West.

Over the last forty or fifty years, while a growing perception developed in the general population that poetry was reserved for a few, the tradition of Western poetry, while probably somewhat diminished, managed to stay alive.

Ever since I started to explore the Northern Range, I've come across people able to recite a poem or two by that old cowboy poet, Anonymous.

Others have showed me poems of their own making. While these didn't always meet conventional literary standards of composition, meter, or even rhyme, they were often entertaining or humorous, and sometimes moving. And there was always delight to be taken from poems that were tales of everyday people: farmers, ranchers, housewives, small-town eccentrics.

The same can be found at the cowboy poetry gatherings held now in virtually every Western state and province. These gatherings, since the first one in Elko, Nevada, in 1985, have sparked renewed interest in Western verse, so much interest that the genre now seems to be flourishing as never before. What impresses me most is the delight people find—in an age of television and videos—in words. It's the kind of delight most people, perhaps, once felt for poetry before it began to be perceived as inaccessible and elitist.

That's why my goal with this anthology has been to select poems that people from the West—especially, perhaps, people who attend cowboy poetry gatherings—might enjoy. I haven't limited the book to poets heard at the gatherings, nor have I tried to make this a collection of "folk" or "cowboy" poems. The test has been that the poems speak to the people of the Northern Range and to people interested in life there. I've limited the selections to this region because it's the place I know best and because it has a common Western heritage despite the international border that divides it.

The Northern Range is where North America saw the last of the open cattle ranges. As those ranges were fenced off—after the Hard Winter of 1886 in Montana, after the even harder winter of 1907 on the Canadian prairies, and after settlement moved even farther north into the last remnants of the open grasslands in later years—a culture emerged that somehow managed to preserve a sense of poetry in its people. This anthology assembles a small portion of that poetry—poetry of the Northern Range.

–*Ted Stone*
*January, 1993*

# FRANK LINDERMAN

*B*orn *in Ohio in 1869, Frank Linderman came west when he was sixteen years old to become a Montana trapper, guide, and then a newspaperman. Among other works, he transcribed reminiscences of the medicine woman Pretty Shield and Chief Plenty Coup of the Crow. Later, he wrote a book of stories of his old friend Charley Russell. The poems that follow are from a collection of Linderman's poems titled* Bunch-Grass and Blue-Joint, *published in 1921.*

# TO THE COYOTE

I uster hate ye once, but now
I've weakened some, an' wonder how
Ye live on airth that's ditched an' fenced,
An' lately, somehow, I've commenced
To like ye.

I uster think ye devil's spawn,
But dang it, all my hate is gone.
I watch ye prowl an' win yer bets
Agin the traps a nester sets
To ketch ye.

Once I practised ornery traits,
An' tempted ye with p'isoned baits;

But if ye'd trust me, an' forgit,
I'd make the play all even yit,
An' feed ye.

It took a time for me to see
What's gittin' you has *landed* me:
Yer tribe, like mine, is gittin' few,—
So let's forgit; an' here's to you,
Ol' timer.

If I could, I'd turn the days
Back to wilder border ways;
Then we'd make our treaty strong,
An' try our best to git along,
Dog-gone ye!

## LUCK

Ol' man Ogletree is smart
    (Got a gizzard fer a heart),
Sez he don't believe in luck,
    Calls it sentimental truck.

Ol' man Ogletree, ye see,
    Owns the "S" and' "Circle-C."
Management, he sez, is what
    Makes the bet an' wins the pot.

Ol' man Ogletree, an' me,

12

In the spring of eighty-three,
Rode the grub-line up the trail
    To the range on Beaver-tail.

Ol' man Ogletree was wild,
    An' a father's only child,
Couldn't ride a wagon-bed,
    Never had a hand ner head;

Wasn't worth a badger's hide
    Till his daddy up an' died,
Leavin' him, alone, ye see,
    With the "S" and' "Circle-C."

# CABINS

They was dirt-roofed, an' homely, an' ramblin', an' squat—
Jest logs with mud-daubin'; but I loved 'em a lot.
Their latch-strings was out, an' their doors wouldn't lock:
Get down an' walk in ('twas politer to knock).
Mebby nobody home, but the grub was all there;
He'p yerse'f, leave a note, to show you was square;
Might be gone for a week; stay as long as you please,
You knowed you was welcome as a cool summer breeze;
Might be spring 'fore you'd see him, then he'd grin an' declare
He'd a-give a good hoss if he'd only been there.
But he's gone with his smile, an' the dear little shack
With his brand on its door won't never come back.
An' his latch-string is hid with the spirit an' ways

That gladdened our hearts in them good early days.
There wasn't a fence in the world that we knew,
For the West an' its people was honest an' new,
And the range spread away with the sky for a lid—
I'm old, but I'm glad that I lived when I did.

# CAYUSE BILL

Old Cayuse Bill was tea'd up right
　　In Shorty's Place the other night,
An', backin' up agin the bar,
　　He hooked his spur on the foot-rail thar
An' moralized on gineral things,
　　From hosses down to queens an' kings.

I've heered it said, an' know it's true,
　　An' like as not you've heered it too,
That, dodgin' all the if's an' but's,
　　It's brains an' not a bunch of guts
That whiskey wakes with idees strange
　　An' with 'em drifts across the range.

"My dad," says Bill, "I never knowed;
　　But jest the same I lived an' growed,
An' I ain't found but what men see
　　An' recognize all good in me,
Without back-trailin' to the ground
　　My parents used to stomp around.

"A thoroughbred in humankind
        Is easy any time to find,
But stake their sons an'—what's the use?
        Nine times in ten they're jest cayuse—
They're throwbacks to forgotten strains
        That run to bone instid of brains.

"A throwback comes a-lopin' in,
        An' like as not he's born a twin
To record-making' breedin' stock;
        But nothing' proves it, 'cept the clock.
He's shy all marks, but jest the same
        He's branded with his daddy's name.

"A strain of blood that's weak an' cold
        May mix with one that's strong an' bold;
An' that cayuse is standard-bred
        That sets his mark a mite ahead,
No matter if his pedigree
        Is known to jest his mother, see?

"Performance," says old Cayuse Bill,
        "Is all that counts, or ever will,
In hosses or in humankind;
        An' every time ye're sure to find
That them that boasts a family tree
        Ain't more'n what they'd oughter be.

"Of course a family's got to start
        Some place, somehow, an' that's the part

Men overlook, until some colt
   Of cayuse stock gives them a jolt
An' cleans 'em up, an' right there he
   Is saved to start a family tree.

"It ain't all breedin', let me state,
   It's this here fast an' fancy gait;
So I have held, pure-bred or cross,
   A man comes standard like a hoss,
By action shown in any game
   To which he lends his strength an' name."

NOTE: *By the law of the turf, a cold-blooded horse may become standard-bred by its own performance.*

# "GIT DOWN AN' COME IN"

"Git down an' come in!"
Could words open wider a heart or a door
Than that greeting of plainsmen in days that are o'er,
"Git down an' come in?"

"Git down an' come in!"
The bid to the stranger, the welcome of friend,
When miles lay ahead, or when nearing an end;
The same in the sunshine, the same in the night:
May mem'ry preserve it, and time never blight
"Git down an' come in!"

# JOHNNY RITCH

*J*ohnny Ritch cowboyed in Montana with Charley Russell in the 1880s. Russell
often said that Ritch's poem "Shorty's Saloon" was his favorite western poem
because it gave the truest picture he knew of a cow-town saloon. Russell liked the
poem so much, in fact, that he illustrated it and gave the work to Ritch as a
gift. All of the poems that follow, including "Shorty's Saloon," appeared in
Ritch's book Horsefeathers.

## SHORTY'S SALOON

By the trails to the Past, on the Plains of No Care,
Stood Shorty's saloon, but now it's not there,
For Shorty moved camp and crossed the Divide
In the years long dim, and naught else beside
A deep brand on Memory brings back the old place,—
Its drinks and its games, and many a face
Peers out from the mists of days that are fled,
When Shorty stood back of his bar, there, and said,
    "What's yours, Pard?"

No fine drinks adorned that primitive bar,
Just "licker" was served, and that seemed by far
The properest stuff in a place, you'll agree,
Where life flowed and ebbed like the tides of a sea,

**17**

Unfettered by care, unmeasured by time,—
Where Innocence formed its first friendships with Crime
Where Bacchus' wild court held ribaldrous sway,
And Shorty, on shift, stood waiting to say,
      "What's yours, Pard?"

Great herds from the South swept by on the trails,
And stages sped Westward, top-heavy with mails
For camps far beyond, where gold was the lust,
And freighters and "bull trains" sent whirlwinds of dust
That scattered and spread far out on the plain,
And men from the wild,—hard men that sin's stain
Had marked like a brand—all stopped there, you see,
And Shorty's brief welcome to each one would be,
      "What's yours, Pard?"

And up from the vast, silent stretch of the range,—
From line camps and roundups, and all of the strange,
Lone places in Cow-land, men came there to play
In that drama whose artists all lived by the way:—
Their sky-line of life blazed crimson and gold,
For hope gave them wealth and youth made them bold
And strong in life's strife to dare any task,
And "licker" was theirs when Shorty would ask
      "What's yours, Pard?"

They danced and they drank, and they sang that old song,
"I'm just a poor cowboy, and know I've done wrong,"
While the click of the chips in the games that were played,
And the sob in the music the violin made

Rang out though the smoke that clouded the room,
For Joy held the top-hand and drink drowned all gloom
The future might hold for him who made gay,—
And life filled with sunbeams, when Shorty would say
      "What's yours, Pard?"

Some tragedies mark those trails to the Past—
Some lone, unnamed graves tell briefly the last
Of the story of those who lived ere the change
From that wild, free life of the Borderless Range,—
But Memory's kind grasp holds gently the place,
Its drinks and its games,—and many a face
Peers out from the mists of days that are fled,
When Shorty stood back of his bar, there, and said,
      "What's yours, Pard?"

# GRUB PILE

Some day some man will write a book
About that gent we called the Cook:

    He'll tell how, in that far back day
    This measly dope held sovereign sway;
    None 'round his tent would risk to say,
    Or even think another way.

Horse wranglers shivered at his word—
Night herders hid behind their herd.

Top hands would never even dare
To cross his path; they'd stand and stare
When Cook's wild eyes began to glare
At some poor fool who'd cussed the fare.

The wagon boss would go and hide—
The Cook was one he couldn't ride.

He knew that cooks were born, not made,—
And roundup cooks that knew their trade
Were glowing pearls and shining jade,
Compared with bums the cafes paid.

The dumbest fool would not dispute
Or cross the will of that galoot.

But when the storm blew bleak and cold,
That coffee pot steamed fragrant gold
From morn to morn—each night he told
The night hawks where the cake was rolled.

Come back, oh, days of sourdough!
Hot cakes like his you'll never know.

A "so and so" boiled in a sack,
With brandy sauce to give it whack!
Who made them like that brainless Jack?
Why were my pants so short on slack?

Who cared if this bloke's head was wood,
He knew his grub—and cooked it good.

Some day we all must make a change
And ride to lands green, new and strange;
And he'll be there,—with sheet-iron range
And all his cussedness and manage,

To hound us with that call so vile,
**"Roll out, you stiffs—roll out,—grub-pile!"**

# THE NIGHT STAGE

"Here comes the Stage," a watcher cries,
The card games end, for all are eyes
To see it stop and learn 'who's on,'—
So quick it comes, so soon is gone.

Thru midnight's gloom it rumbles in,
Old Monte drives,—so tall, so thin—
He grabs the mail sack, heaves it down,
Not much comes to this cow-made town.

The 'fares' unload to have a stretch:
A gambler man, a drink-soaked wretch,
A herder, too,—so old, so gray—
A plump one from the red-light way,

Two young stockmen, a timid Chink.
Old Monte bums his 'station drink,'
Then hurries back, his face all beams,
Stocktender's all thru changing teams.

21

The native group kid Monte some,
A few stand silent, dumb and glum;
He sallies back, then cracks his whip,—
Four salty broncs all plunge and rip,

The gambler man lights his cheroot,
The mail sack's chucked down in the boot,
Like time, like life—each takes its flight—
The Stage rolls on into the night.

# SIGNS

The elks has gone to whistlin' some,
        High on the mountainside;
A blue grouse plays his feath'ry drum
        To lure his ruffled bride.

A wobbly colt romps on the hill,
        An' wee calves frisk and bawl;
Soft evenin' brings it's curdlin' thrill,—
        A wild cat's love-tuned call.

The bustin' buds jest swell an' swell—
        I heered a robin sing—
An', by these signs, I'm here to tell
        The cockeyed world—it's Spring!

# WALLACE DAVID COBURN

*O*ne *of Montana's earliest books of western verse was Wallace David Coburn's* Rhymes of A Round-Up Camp. *Published in 1899 in Great Falls, several of the book's poems became well known throughout the West. Probably the most repeated was "The Stampede," a poem that found its way into oral tradition most often called* It's Hard to Kill a Cowboy.

# THE STAMPEDE

Did you ever hear the story of how one stormy night,
A wild beef herd stampeded, down yonder to the right?
No? Well, you see that sloping hill, beyond the sagebrush flat,
East of the old round-up corral, where all the boys are at?
'Twas one night in November, and I was on first guard;
A storm was brewing in the west, the wind was blowing hard.
Of wild Montana steers we had about a thousand head,
Belonging to the "Circle C," and each one full of "Ned."
The season had been rainy and the grass was thick and long,
So the herd had found good grazing in the hills the whole day long.
The clouds had piled up in the west, a strangely grotesque mass,
And the rain began to patter on the weeds and buffalo grass.
The lightning flared up in the clouds, and all was deathly still,
Except the melancholy howl of a coyote on the hill.
The vivid, shifting lightning kept bright the stormy scene,
And I could see the broken hills, with washouts in between.

And when Bill, who was standing first guard with me that night,
Came jogging past, he 'lowed that it was certainly a sight,
And then commenced to whistle, while I began to sing;
The lightning flared along the sky like demons on the wing.
But round and round rode Bill and me, with slickers buttoned tight,
And looking like dim specters in the constant changing light.
The thunder now began to peal and crash along the sky,
The cattle pawed and moved about, the wind went whistling by.
Then, suddenly, without a sign, there came an awful crash,
And my eyes were almost blinded by a bright and burning flash
That filled the air an instant, then as suddenly went out,
While little sparks of lightning seemed floating all about.
And then the scene that followed defies my tongue to tell,
For those wild steers stampeded when the deadly lightning fell.
I don't know how it happened, but when my vision clears,
I find that I am riding in the midst of running steers.
And, oh! the thoughts that filled my brain as in that living tide
Of hoofs and horns and glowing eyes, I made that fearful ride.
On, on, and on at deadly speed, I dared not slacken pace;
A stone wall could not hinder us in that bloodcurdling race.
And if a cowboy ever prayed with fervor in his prayer,
'Twas me among those madden'd beasts, I prayed in my despair.
My horse was jammed and thrown about as o'er the rocky ground
We sped like some vast torrent, with stubborn, sullen sound.
But when my horse was almost gone, and Death stalked all about,
I heard above the awful roar a cowboy's ringing shout.
And, looking backward in the gloom, I caught a fleeting glance
Of cowboys flitting to and fro, like spirits in a dance.
And then I felt my nerve come back, like some old, long-lost friend,
For I had given up all hope, and waited for the end.
At first I couldn't understand just what they hoped to do,

But soon I saw they meant to cut that running herd in two.
For after cutting off a bunch, they lined up with a cheer,
To form a wedge of solid men and charge them from the rear.
Then on they came through tossing horns, with old Jack in the lead;
The cattle parted stubbornly, but didn't slacken speed.
On and on, with sturdy force, those brave lads struggled on,
But I doubted if they'd reach me before my horse was gone.
For, as I spurred his reeking flanks, and pulled his head up high,
He slowly sank beneath me, and I felt that I must die.
But up again he struggled, then down he went once more,
And I found myself a-knockin' at old Death's gloomy door.
And when I got my senses the hoofs and horns were gone,
And Bill was kneeling at my side with streaming slicker on.
You see, my leg was broken and my chest was badly crushed,
By half a dozen reckless steers, as over me they rushed.
But it's hard to kill a cowboy; they're pretty tough, you know,
Else I'd been riding in the clouds with angels long ago.

# THE COWBOY'S FATE

One night on the fall beef round-up,
    In October of ninety-three,
Jack and I stood guard together—
    This is what he said to me:

"Yes, Bill, times have changed a little,
    Since we first learned how to ride;
Country's full of barbed wire fences,
    And the range is not so wide.

"And, Bill, you are rich and happy,
        Got a wife and lots of gold;
Been a man and stuck to business,
        While I—well, I'm getting old.

"Yes, I've been in many places,
        Sorter on the French qui vive;
Wouldn't get but just located,
        When I'd up and have to leave.

"Have to pack my bed and vanish;
        Pull out for the high divide;
Seek a new range, strike a cow ranch,
        Settle down and try to ride.

"Get a good job on the roun-up;
        Make a stake and go to town,
There fill up on Injun whiskey,
        Pull my gun and saunter 'roun'.

"Smoke the town and whip the sheriff,
        Play 'em high, and shoot and shout,
Till the air was filled with music
        And the people all hid out.

"Then I'd saddle up my private,
        Fog the street lights on the run,
Till I struck the open prairie—
        Then my painting job was done.

"That is why I'm here tonight, Bill;
       Ridin' 'roun' this old beef herd,
Listening to the coyotes holler—
       Echoes of the life I've blurred.

"And it seems like luck's against me,
       Now that I am getting gray;
For you know the good old sayin',
       'Every dog will have his day.'

"I can't stand the hard knocks now, Bill,
       That I used to think was fun;
And I'm like an old cow pony
       That's forgotten how to run.

"Say, Bill; you may think I'm nervy,
       Wouldn't ask if I was flush,
But a man can't stan' to winter
       Like a dogie in the brush.

"And I thought I'd better ask, Bill,
       If you'd let me have a show
Just to earn a winter's grub stake,
       Even if it's shovelin' snow.

"For, you see, I ain't partic'lar
       What I drive at nowadays,
Just to earn an honest livin',
       For it's steady work that pays.

"And a man can't make a fortune
  Paintin' towns and gettin' drunk;
Tried it long enough to know, Bill;
  Wish I'd all the coin I've sunk.

"Thanks; I knew 'twould be a cold day
  When you wouldn't help me, Bill;
Didn't know jest where I'd winter,
  And the weather's gettin' chill.

"These nights makes a feller wonder
  Where his summer work has gone,
When the frost sticks to his whiskers,
  And he needs a coonskin on.

"Hope we'll have a few more warm days,
  Till we get these cattle shipped,
For this wind cuts like a blizzard,
  Makes me feel like I'd been whipped.

"Two o'clock! Well, who'd 'a' thought it?
  Time has flew on angel's wings,
As I heard an eastern feller
  Tell a girl down at the Springs.

"So, I guess I'd better hurry
  And wake up the next relief—
Guess a camp's over in that coulee,
  Just beyond the rocky reef.

"So long, Bill; I'll see you later!"
        And old Jack passed out of sight;
Gayly singing as he galloped
        To his death that stormy night.

For we found his lifeless body
        When the morning sun arose,
With the diamond frost still sparkling
        On his blood be-spattered clothes.

For, you see, his horse had fallen;
        Struck a hole, and Jack was caught,
With his head crushed on a boulder—
        Thus his tragic death was wrought.

Poor old Jack! Good-hearted always,
        May his soul in peace abide,
Where good cowboys ride in comfort,
        Far beyond the "Great Divide."

# SUNRISE IN THE BAD LANDS

The dawn is breaking in the east,
    Above the Bad Land hills;
An early rising camp-bird sweet
    His morning carol trills.

A rabbit darts behind a bush,
    And sits in comic pose
To gaze with startled eyes at one
    Of bunnie's human foes.

The month is crisp November, and
    The brown earth calmly sleeps
Beneath the pure white mantle, that
    Upon her bosom heaps.

The campfire smoke goes curling out
    Upon the morning breeze,
With rare and grotesque forms that float
    Among the leafless trees.

The timid deer comes down to drink
    And play upon the sand,
Along the old Missouri's bank,
    So picturesque and grand.

Then suddenly from out her bed,
    The sun breaks into view;
To bid the world good-morrow with
    A greeting ever new.

# ROBERT FLETCHER

*R*obert Fletcher was born in Iowa in 1885 and came to Montana in the early years of this century. A writer of diverse talents, he wrote, among several books and articles, the original lyrics for the song "Don't Fence Me In"— and then sold them to Cole Porter for $250. His books of Western verse, Prickly Pear Poems and Corral Dust, from which these poems are taken, were published in 1920 and 1934.

## RINGBONE SAM

This library over at Malta
That Carnegie done staked them to,
I reckon they're all mighty proud of,
She bein' so gala and new.
They tell me she's chuck full of readin',
She bulges with unabridged tomes
With history, art, and with science,
With lyrics, with prose, and with poems.

Now some folks for books has a cravin'
While to others they don't mean a damn,
But stranger, you talk about book sharps,
The high card is ol' Ringbone Sam.
This yere Ringbone, he hasn't no schoolin'

Or no intellectual look,
But, pard, talk about education!
He acquires it all out of one book.

He cherishes that valued volume,—
Peruses her faithful and true,—
Say, I jest wish that I had a dollar
For each time he's done read her through.
She's got pictures from cover to cover
And Ringbone, he knows 'em by heart,—
Why, to show you the value of readin'
You jest let an argument start.

Some evein' down at the bunkhouse,—
You know how them cowpunchers get,—
And Ringbone is ast for his judgment,
He settles it, that's a sure bet.
He can discourse, pard, somethin' amazin'—
His knowledge is varied and keen,—
He's authority sure on his subjeck,—
That sport packs a heap in his bean.

Now if one book disseminates wisdom
So copious like and so free,
Jest imagine this yere Ringbone person
Absorbin' of two, or of three!
But Ringbone is jest as contented,—
One book suits him, he ain't no hawg,—
But he sure loves that sheep herder's bible,—
Montgomery Ward's catalog.

# THE TRAIL OF AN OLD TIMER'S MEMORY

There's a trail that leads out to the mountains
Through the prairie dust velvety gray,
Through the canyons, the gulches, and coulees,
A trail that grows dimmer each day.
You can't make it without an old timer
To guide you and make you his guest,
For that trail is the long trail of memory—
And it leads to the heart of the West.

Now it winds through the shadows of sorrow,
Now it's warmed by the sunlight of smiles,
Now it lingers along pleasant waters,
Now it stretches o'er long, weary miles.
But it never is lonesome, deserted,
As you journey its distances vast
For it always is crowded and peopled
With dim phantom shapes of the past.

Freight wagons creaking and lurching
Leaving the old trading posts,
And Indian war parties scouting
As silent and furtive as ghosts;
Cowpunchers driving the trail herd,
The stage coach that swayed as she rolled
With her passengers, sourdough and pilgrim,
In quest of adventure and gold.

Cavalry trots through the dust clouds,

Hunter and trapper and scout,
Miner and trader and outlaw
All meet on this marvelous route
Where laughter and tears are found mingled,
Where a prince may be found in a shack,
On this trail to the days 'most forgotten,
The days that will never come back.

# THE MISSOURI

Yes, stranger, I came up that river
Back in the old early days
And I've sure got a strong likin' for her,—
She's human-like, pard, in her ways.
Where them summer clouds 'most touch the snow banks,—
Spread like linen to bleach in the sun,—
While the mountain flowers bloom on their borders,—
Where them little rills tickle and run.

Till bounding down through the canyons
With pennants of mist all unfurled
A thousand bold streams came a leaping
Off the eaves of the roof of the world,—
In the land of the geysers and glaciers
Where the hills have been battered and torn
By mysterious hands, in their making,
That there river Missouri was born.

Some rivers are smiling and happy,

Some rivers are sullen and grim,
Some rivers remind you of ragtime
While some have the sound of a hymn.
Some saunter along at their leisure,
Some brawl as they rush on their way,
The Missouri? Well, she's kind of diff'rent
From the rest of them, I'm here to say.

Now maybe the reason I like her,
The reason I think she's the best,
The friendliest, strongest, and biggest,
Is because she's a part of the West.
A highway that led from the eastward
To a country of sapphire and gold,
A trail that allured with a promise
The hearts of the strong and the bold.

But those days are now gone forever,
I'd sure like to live them again,
Those days of real joy and real sorrow,
Those days of real women and men.
And I'll bet the Missouri is lonesome
As I am for those early days,
For the both of us sure are old timers
And she's human-like, pard, in her ways.

# MIKE LOGAN

*P*hotographer-writer Mike Logan has appeared at cowboy poetry gatherings throughout the United States and Canada. His poems stem from his interest in Western history and experiences photographing life on Montana ranches. In addition to three books of photographs, Logan has published two volumes of verse, Bronc to Breakfast *and* Laugh Kills Lonesome, *from which the following poems are taken.*

## BEHOLD A PALE HORSE

*"And I looked, and behold a pale horse: and his name that sat on him was Death, and Hell followed with him."* Revelations 6:8

Montana 1886
A pale horse first appears.
White shadow on a drought-struck range.
The coldest fall in years.

That horse he first was sighted
Up north on Crooked Creek,
The day the year's worst storm blew in
And howled for more 'n a week.

He seemed some awful phantom.
Some harbinger of doom.
That pale horse lopin' cold and gaunt
Through winter's gatherin' gloom.

Most outfits wintered cows that year
That usu'lly they'd a sold,
'Cause cattle prices dropped so far
That cowmen chanced the cold.

He ghosted down the Musselshell
Behind a warm chinook.
Froze sheaths of ice on all the grass
With just his pale-eyed look.

That horse loped towards the Judith
And filled that range with dread
'Cause, where he went, great blizzards struck
And whole cowherds lay dead.

He worked his evil 'cross the plains
And up the Little Dry.
Wreaked havoc as he passed that way.
More herds laid down to die.

It got to where, to cut his track
Filled cowmen's hearts with fear
As coulees clogged with starvin' cows
That grim and direful year.

Cowhands lost toes and fingers
As they fought to save their herds.
The sight of cattle dyin' slow
Was pain too fierce for words.

That horse's passin' iced the streams
And thirst crazed steers broke through
And drowned as others pushed 'em in.
Weren't nothin' Man could do.

When spring, it finally came that year
Old timers still take vows
That men could walk for miles and miles
On carcasses of cows.

The Hell that followed with that horse
Was in the eyes of men
Who'd rolled the dice with nature
And seen their life's dreams end.

They called it, The Hard Winter.
It blew the winds of change,
When Death he rode a pale horse
And killed the open range.

# RANCH TRUCK

A ranch truck's like a rancher.
Don't dress up fit t' kill.
Just goes an' gets the job done
Without no pomp or frill.

While they ain't long on beauty,
Ranch trucks can hold their own.
Just see if this ol' pickup
Don't sound like some you've known.

Me an' Bruce hop in his pickup.
We got some hay to load.
He's got 'er chained on all four wheels
'Cause last night it shore snowed.

Hayhooks festoon the gearshift.
There's stockwhips on the seat.
Ol' Skipper's on the towchains
That's piled beneath my feet.

The windshield's cracked an' muddy.
I give ol' Skip a shove.
The dash wears thirteen mittens
An' one odd left-hand glove.

It also sports three hammers,
Two pairs of fencin' pliers,
A stick 'r two of kindlin'
From last spring's brandin' fires,

Five caps an' some old glasses,
A Pepsi can 'r two,
A box of mixed up nuts an' bolts
An' one old workhorse shoe.

There's binder twine an' ear tags,
Some strings wound on a spool,
A can of pills for calf scours
An' a new ear taggin' tool,

A shot 'r two of Longicil,
A length of rawhide thong,
A pair of ancient channel locks,
A tape just ten feet long,

A crescent wrench, a pill gun,
Band-Aids, a chain saw file,
Three scarves an' one old down vest
All wadded in a pile,

Six washers on a twist of wire,
Eight cents in cold hard cash,
A clevis, a direction book,
An' that's just on the dash.

Between us there's two sacks of cake,
Three jackets an' some chaps,
A slicker an' a Swede saw
An' three new leadrope snaps.

The floor holds one old halter,
An ax, two pairs of spurs,
A head stall an' two oil cans
An' a blanket full of burrs,

Some gunnysacks, a brandin' iron,
A brand new ropin' rope,
A pair of irrigatin' boots
An' a bar of Lava soap.

No tellin' what's behind the seat.
I'm sure ol' Bruce cain't say,
But we won't worry 'bout what's there
'Cause it ain't in the way.

We lost a tally book last week.
I'm 'fraid we're out of luck.
It's prob'ly lost forever
In Bruce's ol' red truck.

Sounds like I'm knockin' Bruce's truck?
Well, that'd be plumb mean.
'Sides, we thought of usin' my rig,
But it ain't half that clean.

# LAUGH KILLS LONESOME

He called it LAUGH KILLS LONESOME.
Shows old friends around the fire
An' them boys is swappin' windys
Long before they savvied wire.

Charlie stands there in the firelight.
He's the nighthawk who's rode in.
He, mostly, talked to hosses.
Sang nightsongs to the wind.

That paintin' shows another time
When men rode all alone
An' yarnin' by the cookfire
Made a wagon seem like home.

You can feel ol' Charlie mournin'.
He'd 'a give up wealth an' fame
To ride back down them old trails
Before the land was tame.

LAUGH KILLS LONESOME, Charlie loved it,
That time now long ago,
When the wind still blew, unfettered,
From the Milk to Mexico.

# GAGGLES 'N GANGS, McCARTYS 'N HANGS

We had a vis'tor at the ranch,
This gent he was a "Limey,"
And the names he gave t' critters,
They sounded plumb old timey.

He said turkeys roam in "rafters"
And pheasants in "bouquets"
And larks in "exaltations,"
While squirrels, they climb in "drays."

"If you look where these names come from,"
Said he, "You're sure to see
What, in fifteenth century England,
They called 'Books of Courtesy.'"

"They tried to give each group of beasts
A proper nomenclature,
That's socially acceptable,
When one discusses nature,"

Now when his lordship took his leave,
I thought I'd try my hand
At givin' bunches on the range
Some names we'd understand.

If geese all glide in "gaggles"
And elk, they graze in "gangs,"
Do you think it might be possible

That rustlers swung in *hangs*?

And if fish all swim in "schools"
And dogs, they run in "packs,"
Would you think it plumb surprisin'
If saddles bunched in *kacks*?

If moles all dig in "labors"
And jays, they form a "party,"
Do you s'pose a bunch of lead ropes
Might braid up a *McCarty*?

If you hear a "charm" of finches
Or a "parliament" of owls
Is there any way that families
Of coyotes could be *howls*?

If you see some swine in "sounders"
Could broncs, they fight in *bucks*
Or groups of irrigators
Go out to work in *mucks*?

If you find a "knot" of hoptoads
Or a plover "congregation,"
Could roosts of trouble makin' crows
Be dubbed an *aggravation*?

If turtles, they all crawl in "bales"
And apes, they're called a "shrewdness,"
Could a crew of drunken cowhands
Be labeled as a *crudeness*?

Could polecats waft in *pungencies*
Or sheep get trimmed in *shears*
Or rock chucks feed in *munches*
Or wolves, they hunt in *weres?*

Could lambs, they go in *gambols*
Or cougars slink in *prowls*
Or bees all buzz in *bumbles*
Or spurs hang up in *rowels?*

Could heifers turn *Houdinis*
As they slip between the wires
Or punchers slouch in *windies*
When they're yarnin' 'round the fires?

Could hawks, they mouse in *hovers*
Or bulls, they form a *beller*
Or magpies make a *mischief*
Or auctioneers a *seller?*

This word game's run away with me.
I'm plumb confused at times.
If cowboy poets, frosted up
Would they recite in *rimes?*

Well, friends, I think you get my drift.
This went from bad to worse.
'Sides, I know them cowboy poets
Would rather form a *verse.*

# WALLACE MCRAE

*Wallace McRae began writing poetry over twenty-five years ago. Today, he recites his work regularly on a syndicated television program,* The West. *He has performed at cowboy poetry gatherings, at the National Cowboy Poetry Hall of Fame, and other venues throughout the West and as far afield as Australia. He is also the first cowboy poet to be granted a National Heritage Award in Washington, D.C. McRae also manages his family's 30,000 acre cow-calf operation near Forsyth, Montana.*

## NATIONAL PARK

One year with haying over, when we wasn't fighting water,
I gather up the family, sayin' "Folks I think we aughter
Take a short vacation. Fly off like a meaderlark
We'll relax some like civilians in a scenic Nashnul Park."
So we pack half the stuff we own in our flap-fendered car
And hit the trail for mountains that beckon from afar.
Well, we gets there in a day or so, with a minimum of fuss,
When we gets there, half the world's there too. In line ahead of us.
'Course all our bedrolls are to home. Ain't no place for us to stay.
The Ranger says the bears'd git us if we slept out anyway.
So we retreat, again' the grain, halfway home to some bed ground.
And contrary to all instincts, next morning turn around
And take another run. This time we're lead wolves in the pack.

The drag is challenging us leaders and there ain't no turnin' back!
Well there's hoards of humans waitin' at every scenic spot
And we can't get outa traffic though our radiator's hot.
We seen new sights like sun bounced off'n lines of cars plumb blinding
And heard the eerie mating call of 'lectric cameras winding.
Heard languages from places a damn long ways from here.
Saw license plates from states that I've forgot for forty year.
And git ups? Lord a mighty! on every shape and size of bod.
While me, wearin' what I always wear, they eye me like I'm odd!
They got words writ on their T-shirts that I know's again' the law,
That I read from 'neath my hat brim, hopin' no one seen I saw.
Oh, we saw rocks 'n trees and streams. We seen some waterfall.
But mostly we seen humans. Watched 'em mill 'n paw 'n bawl.
We straggled home crowd-foundered from our Park experience.
Plumb wore out like we'd branded calves, or built a mile a' fence.
You can bet your last calf check any rock pile that is steep'll
(And is called some kind of Park'll) be overrun with people.
So when we see them pretty pictures of them Parks and yearn to roam,
We think about them millin' herds and stay the hell to home.

# SHOPPING

Dang near every Tuesday I go and watch the cattle sell
Down at the local sale barn. I sit with Buster Fell.
Me and Buster, we go way back. Since kids, well, we been friends.
Buster 'n me keeps up on things; politics 'n cattle trends.
We never bid on cattle. Don't need nothin', him or me.
Then we eat a bite at Gert's Cafe; Maybe drink a tall ice tea.
I 'most always eats The Special. Buster has the chicken fried.

We talk about the high school teams, good horses and who died.
Now lately, Clara, she's the wife, she wants to go with me.
Says she wants to do some shopping with Buster's Anna Lee.
"Whatcha need? I'll get it." First time out I volunteer.
"I just want to do some shopping," she says as if she didn't hear.
"For what? I said I'd buy it. Save you a trip to town."
"Buy what?" she says. "Buy what you need," I says 'n sorta frown.
'Fore I knows that there's a problem, it's Katie-bar-the-door.
We pawed up dirt 'n rattled horns for an hour or maybe more.
I ask her nice, "What's eatin' you?" Her control's about to fail.
"It's you and Buster, Gert's Cafe; and the stupid auction sale."
I tells her, "Hon, that's business. You surely savvy that.
I gotta stay on top of things; know where the market's at."
"Do you buy anything?" she says. "Just supper," I replied.
"It's just like shopping then," she says. 'N I'm plumb mystified.

We patched things up. We hugged. She cried. But I ain't got a clue
Of what it is we fought about, but once a week we two
Meet Buster and his missus in the sale barn parking lot.
The women they go into town, but by evening they ain't bought
No more'n me 'n Buster has, 'cept for groceries and stuff,
But they seem to have a high old time, which I guess is fair enough.
We all four eats at Gert's Cafe, talk of weddings, showers and drought,
But I ain't got them women 'n their shopping figgered out.

# A CONVERSATION WITH ALBERT

"My predecessors were pioneers,
You see, well over a hundred years
Have passed since John B. lit here, fresh off the Texas trail."
I thought old Albert'd be impressed.
He sorta gazed off t'wards the west
I took that for encouragement, and I went on with my tale.
"The land was young, just like John B.,
The water good, the grass was free.
The Army and the railroad combined to open up the land.
The wolf was here, but the buffalo
No longer wandered to and fro,
So a man could make a living running stock. You understand?"
Albert nodded, and then he said,
"I understand, you go ahead
And tell me of your hist'ry. I should learn it," and he smiled.
I said, "The first ones here, they had it best
'Til the grangers came and plowed and messed
The country with their fences; and tamed the land once wild.
Though they were diff'rent, farmers weren't no fools.
They built communities and roads and schools
And churches. And I guess that has all been for the best.
But they plowed land a man can't trust.
When it got dry, they all went bust.
But they somehow killed the culture of the old-time cowboy West.
Oh, there's still cowboys in picture shows
On the TV tube and at rodeos,
But no one really understands that a way of life was lost.
We got welfare now, and laws and rules

From the government, enforced by fools.
We're losing pride and independence, and that's an awful cost.
We've traded off pride for the role
Of a prostitute. We're on the dole
Of every give-away program that comes rollin' down the road.
I suppose we realized
That everybody's subsidized
And we dang sure oughta get our share! Forget the rancher code.
It's been a long time—a hundred years—
But it seems to me, my ancestors' fears
Are coming back to haunt me, and dang it that ain't right.
It's too late in this modern day
We shoulda fought it, back along the way.
Hell, I bet we'd prob'ly won it, if we'd put up a fight!"
"You might," says Albert. "I wouldn't know.
But maybe not. I gotta go.
So long, and I sympathize with your situation."
With a "See you," and a "You take care"
Albert Tallbull left me standing there.
And drove off nice and easy back to his Reservation.

# GIVE US A SONG, IAN TYSON

Write me a tune, Ian Tyson,
With a beat sort of easy and slow
That will flow down each valley and canyon
From Alberta to Old Mexico.
Make it sound like the wind in the pine trees
Or the plains muffled deep in the snow.

Yes, please, write me a tune, Ian Tyson,
Like an old one the cowboys all know.

Write down some words, Ian Tyson,
Words that put a sad tear in my eye.
Words that speak of the unspoken yearning
That I have for the old days gone by.
Tell again of our shame, or our glory,
With a shout, or perhaps with a sigh.
Won't you write down some words, Ian Tyson,
Of the West, 'neath a big open sky.

Sing me your song, Ian Tyson,
Would you sing your song only for me?
Let the ripples of music transport me
Like the waves carry ships on the sea.
Make me fight, or just languidly listen.
Sing of strife, or of sweet harmony.
But please sing me your song, Ian Tyson,
Sing it softly, and easy and free.

Teach us your song, Ian Tyson,
So the cowboys can all sing along.
And forgive when we stumble and mumble
Or when we get the verses all wrong.
It's your fate to be placed as the hero
Of a bowlegged buckaroo throng.
So we'll borrow your song, Ian Tyson,
And then call it our own cowboy song.

They'll steal your song, Ian Tyson,
Steal the song that the cowboys love well.
And they'll change both the beat and the lyrics
Then they'll merchandise it with hard sell.

@KUET HAFSO '93

# PAUL ZARZYSKI

*P*aul Zarzyski, from Augusta, Montana, used to travel the professional rodeo circuit riding bareback broncs. These days, Zarzyski rides the "poetry trail," giving readings and teaching workshops. The following poems are from his latest book, Roughstock Sonnets.

# THE HEAVYWEIGHT CHAMPION PIE-EATIN' COWBOY OF THE WEST

I just ate 50 pies—started off with coconut
macaroon, wedged my way through bar angel
chocolate, Marlborough, black walnut and sour cream
raisin to confetti-crusted crab apple—
still got room for dessert
and they can stick their J–E–L–L–O
where the cowpie don't' shine, cause Sugar Plum
I don't eat nothing made from horses' hooves!

So make it something *pie,* something light
and fancy, like huckleberry fluffy chiffon, go
extra heavy on the hucks and fluff—beaten
egg whites folded in *just* so. Or let's shoot
for something in plaid, red and tan lattice-
topped raspberry, honeyed crust

flakey and blistered to a luster, wild
fruit oozing with a scoop of hard vanilla!

Or maybe I'll strap on a feedbag of something
a smidgen more timid: quivering
custard with its nutmeg-freckled fill
nervous in the shell. Come to think of it now,
blue ribbon mincemeat sounds a lot
more my cut: neck of venison, beef suet,
raisins, apples, citrus peel, currants—
all laced, Grammy-fashion, in blackstrap molasses!

No. Truth is, I'm craving shoofly or spiced rhubarb
or sure hard to match peachy praline,
cinnamon winesap apple à la mode, walnut
crumb or chocolate-frosted pecan. *OR*,
whitecapped high above its fluted deep-dish crust,
a lemon angel meringue—not to mention
mandarin apricot, black bottom, banana cream,
burgundy berry or Bavarian nectarine ambrosia!

And how could you out-gun the Turkeyday
old reliables: sweet potato, its cousin
pumpkin, its sidekicks Dutch apple and cranberry
ice cream nut. Ah, harvest moon, that autumn
gourmet cheese supreme, or Jack Frost squash, or…
"my favorite," you ask? That's a tough one.
Just surprise me with something new, Sweetie
Pie—like tangerine boomerang gooseberry!

# RODEO-ROAD FOUNDER:
# HIGHWAY HORSEPLAY

Say horses were elk, and elk
horses: eyes around every elkshoe
curve would pack more weight, spook me
worse, and I'd be glued to the wheel, pulling
leather all night long, from Alberta, to Cranbrook
B.C., Sandpoint, Coeur d'Alene...after 8
hang-and-rattle seconds—spur to antler—
locking horns with a bucking wapiti.

Say elk were horses, and horses
elk: it's a long, hard haul after all but 1
of your 9 lives flash before your eyes
aboard a bugling cayuse, especially
when you draw old Velvet Double 7,
triple rank, his royal head of ivory
tines stabbing, battering you
half to death and senseless.

Say horses were elk, and elk
horses: caution
sign language would change in silhouette
and mustang eyes would shift
at different gaits from borrow pits
to the center of your lane. Daybreak,
you'd see compact cars, not ungulates
chassis-up and driving magpies mad.

Say elk were horses, and horses
elk: you'll say anything, won't you,
you knee-jerkin', suicide-circuit-
chasin' maniac of a loon—any singsong
screwball thing to stay alive when you're dead
tired, gassin' and mashin' it,
gettin' your holts and yodelin' down the road
rodeo to rodeo to rodeodeodeo...

# CUTTING THE EASTER COLT

This saddlebag surgeon readies his tools
like a Monsignor prepares
        for communion. Holy day or not,
nothing's sacrilegious
        when the moon comes
ripe, the disinfectant fumes
        stunning us hard as incense
at high mass. We lead
        the stud, procession-like, into the corral,
scotch-hobble and throw him
        fast with cotton ropes, then watch
this wrangler/pastor/sawbones—all-
        arounder—move his 55 years of heart
and savvy, lickety-split
        amid thrashing hooves
to lash all 4 together
        at the pasterns. He swashes
the scrotum, a glistening lobed

world, delicate and thin-veined—perfect
contrast to his saddlemaker hands,
      fingers braided like rawhide bosals,
his knuckles the thick heel knots.

      With knife honed to a featheredge,
he makes the incision and probes
      until he hunts both down,
an Easter egg apiece for the blue
      heeler pups, their anxious panting
reflected in the gold
      chalice of the gelding's eye.

# FINALE

The iron drives this bay mare
crazy from chute 8, rowels zinging
like thumbnail-size flies
in fever heat, that sudden bite
and ring behind her ears
again and again, spurring every jump
and kick. She buries her head
blind between her knees,
hits the fence head-on,
wire mesh heaving. Her neck
snaps above the withers
where the rider feels life go
in one quick explosion of dust.
Mesh collapses like lung wall
on that last long breath. She tumbles
and shakes, the grandstand
stone-still, the cowboy pinned,
his face to her muzzle—hard
grimace to petrified stare.
And through that deep purple spectrum
end of pain, her nostrils
blossom pink and renegade
as wild rose, a single
springtime applause
in a graveyard of rimrock.

# GWEN PETERSEN

*Gwen Petersen lives on a small ranch near Big Timber, Montana. Known primarily for her humor, in books such as* The Ranch Woman's Manual, The Greenhorn's Guide to the Woolly West, *and* In The Sidesaddle, *Petersen writes from both a rural and feminine perspective. The two poems following come from her book* A Tall Bush: Ranch Woman Rhymes.

## WOMAN OF THE LAND

Her name won't be in history books,
This woman of the land,
Her heart is where it wants to be,
Content with heaven's plan.

And in the corridors of time,
Her way is counted true;
Enduring hardships, strong as rock,
She does what she must do.

Born when wire had begun
To stitch up prairie seams;
When homesteads patched the Western Land—
Quilts of hope-filled dreams.

A herder's wagon was her home
In sun or rain or wind;
She and Pa did outside work,
While Sis and Ma stayed in.

Her Pa hired out his greyhound dogs
To track the coyotes down;
With hounds in cages, he would drive
From ranch to farm to town.

Pa never settled down for long,
For when the bounty slowed,
They packed the wagons, hitched the teams,
And traveled down the road.

Sometimes Pa would trade for goods
Like shoes for her or Sis;
And once he got a violin,
Its song was like a kiss.

But Pa resold the fiddle for
Another purebred hound.
She watched it go without a word
And cried without a sound.

They lived awhile at Charlo's house,
The Flathead tribal chief;
A gentle man and kind, she says,
Who never showed his grief.

In hand-me-downs she walked for miles
To learn to read and write;
For school was just a sometime thing.
Wherever Pa would light.

But when she reached her sixteenth year,
She caught a cowboy's eye;
He asked her would she marry him—
And make him apple pie.

As partner, double-harnessed now
She worked beside her man;
They saved and bought a modest spread.
And settled on their land.

She toiled in cold and snow and wet
Or heat that scorched her bones;
No 'lectric lights to chase the dark,
No plumbing in their home.

She saw the land was good and strong
And planned to run some sheep;
And when he called her fool, she said,
"Those woolies I will keep."

They cared for cattle side by side
Though sheep were hers alone;
But in the fall, the lamb checks paid
The interest on the loan.

Then Nature dealt another hand—
A child was due in May;
And though it didn't slow her much,
She did take off one day.

The baby boy was strong until
Pneumonia won the fight;
The child was buried on their land,
She battled grief at night.

Then, trailing cows, her pony fell
In crashing crushing pile;
Her belly took the saddlehorn,
And town was thirty mile.

Her cowboy found her, took her in;
To God he made a plea.
They patched her up, her scars grew dim,
But, children weren't to be.

She poured her spirit into work
On land that gave—and took;
She held no grudge and never cast
A single backward look.

As years slipped by in River Time
Her cowboy lost his sight;
They sold the ranch and bought a place
More suited to his plight.

One day he started 'cross the road,
She shouted—caught her breath
Her cowboy never saw the car
That dashed him to his death.

And now she ran the ranch alone
And with her partner gone;
The only thing remaining true—
The land was there each dawn.

As time and strength began to wane,
She took another chance;
And bought a tiny piece of earth—
A widow-woman's ranch.

There's sheep and rabbits, goats for milk,
And hens for eggs or stew;
She doesn't wait for other folks
To tell her what to do.

She's planted trees to shade the house,
And sowed some grass for hay;
She irrigates her rocky patch,
Stays busy through the day.

Her hands are gnarled, her step is slow,
Yet when she's asked to town
By kindly Senior Center folks,
She always turns them down.

"I haven't time, I've chores," she says,
"They're what I aim to do,
My heart is where it wants to be
My land will see me through."

Though her name won't be in history books
And her range is less than grand;
Her heart is where it wants to be—
This Woman of the Land.

# THAT DAD-BLAMED WIND

The wind in Upper Yellowstone can blow horrendous gales;
It whistles oe'r the mountain tops with lonesome banshee wails;
No man, no woman, child nor beast can stand against its force,
That dreadful scalping wind can blast a boxcar off its course.

You walk half-bent, your head hunched down, a hand upon your hat,
And if the wind should stop a sec, you're apt to fall, kersplat!
The fellers standing 'round in groups just chewing on their snoose,
Are careful not to spit up-wind for fear of freckle juice.

The wind peels paint from house and barn, plays dice with giant rocks;
Its wild-beast voice can even make a preacher cuss his flocks.
It forces trees and plants to lean with branches to one side,
And all the cats have had their fur sand-blasted off their hides.

The hens jigtime a two-step dance a-slant the awful breeze;
A rooster aims but overshoots a feathered barnyard tease.

And cattle drift before the bluster, pushed to exodus
By wind that sticks its icy claws in every orifice.

Remorseless, wailing, piercing, shrieking, never-stopping howls,
Hyenas make those kinds of sounds when emptying their bowels.
And horses linger, heads hung low and stoically withstand
The freezing frigid frenzied furies sweeping cross the land.

And kids get lifted off their feet and blown to Grandma's digs;
But she's gone bald because the wind has snatched away her wig.
And junior shoves a crowbar through a knothole in the fence;
It quivers there and slowly bends before the turbulence.

But I for one have had it with the raw and chilling wind;
It blows me helter-skelter till I don't know where I've been;
When I retire I do not want the trade winds kissing me;
No drafts, no puffs, no breezes please, on my anatomy.

Just give me temperature that's mild and sun that is superb,
Where birds and bees don't lose their wings in gales of ninety per;
And let me bask in flowery bower and wander on the grass,
And the only wind displeasing comes—from someone passing gas.

# AFTON BLOXHAM

*A fton Bloxham has written a book of poems and published numerous arti-cles for newspapers and journals. Most of her poems come from the obser-vations and experiences she has had ranching near Wilsall, Montana.*

## THE SETTLERS

When out riding, did you ever find a homestead in the hills,
with its boards all cracked and rotting, no glass at the sills?
Did you stop there just to ponder, to look around awhile?
Did you let their spirits enter yours and greet them with a smile?
Did you see the sagging lean-to with its shingles blown away?
Could you smell the yellow roses still blooming there today?

If you sat a spell out on the porch, I'll bet you saw his dream
of cattle grazing on the hills, of horses near the stream.
I'll bet you felt her presence there, standing tall and strong.
Proud to have some land to own, to stay their whole life long.

Did you feel their heartbeats quicken as the Indians came 'round?
Note the way their hearing picked up every little sound?
Could you hear their quiet sobbing as they laid their child to rest?
Could you sense the empty hollow that she held within her breast?
Were their faces lined with worry when the drought came year by year?
Were the winters long and frigid, and the cross too hard to bear?

**66**

Do you think that its their headstones up on the hill nearby?
Do you think they *chose* their resting place beneath Montana's sky?

It's like walking in their footsteps with a firm and steady tread,
for their phantom spirits linger to guard the old homestead.

## HAYIN'

Hayin' season. What a pain!
Two whole months you pray for rain,
But it's dry as it can be.
Not one drop of rain you see—
Until you get the first field mowed.
Then clouds move in and drop their load.

Hayhands, anxious, watch the sky,
Seein' unpaid hours go by.
Sun comes out and there's a breeze.
Moods improve, ulcers ease.
Swathers, balers head out soon.
Some of them break down by noon.

Shear bolts bust off one by one,
Rollers jam, gears won't run.
Knotters quit—they just won't tie.
When they're fixed the hay's too dry!
Bale at night when there's some dew,
Neck is stiff, back aches too.
Hired help is hard to please,
One hates carrots, one hates peas.

One says chicken's all he'll eat,
One devours all that's sweet.
Mercury rises—day by day.
Temperatures and tempers lay
One degree away from blow.
It's getting done—but, oh, so slow!

It's toil and struggle, strain and sweat
To keep things runnin' right—and yet,
Time will come when all we hear
Is how the hay got done—this year!

## SPRING DRIVE

We were trailin' cow and calves
To upper pastures one spring day.
The melt was runnin' heavy,
With green grass along the way.

The road lay turned and twisted
Like a ribbon in the breeze,
And the fence was sagged and broken
From deep snow and winter freeze.

Old cows, their destination
From years past, were hot to go,
But their babies tired quickly
And made the travel slow.

Now and then, when all was quiet,
And linin' out real fine,
And the cowboys were a-lazin',
Half asleep in warm sunshine

Some ornery little critter
Gets his tail hindside before,
Shifts gears until he's jet propelled.
He's headed home for sure.

Two or three more try to follow,
But the riders pull up fast,
And the dogies get a lesson
From a cowhand's rope, well cast.

When you think that things are easin'
And the herd is movin' well,
Some hair-brained city slicker
Scatters them to—Well,

The idiot comes honkin'
And a-roarin' from the rear,
Pushin' calves right through the fences
As he revs into low gear.

Now I'm a gentle woman,
Not given much to ire,
But this thoughtless, cocky driver
Set a spark beneath my fire.

So I rode up to his window
And said, "Mister, I'll allow
Any fool can drive an auto,
But *it takes brains to drive a cow!"*

# THE LAST RITES

Abe and Myrt lived north of town
on a little old ranch he'd let run down.
With Myrt obese and ailing, too
it seemed to Abe all he could do,
with eight boys growing lean and tall,
was scratch and scrape to feed them all.

In summer Abe's old pick-up truck,
with lots of cussin' and some luck,
could haul one pup, eight kids, six bales,
and travel with the speed of snails.

But when it turned to rain and snow
that sometimes reached forty below,
he needed something big and cheap
to tote the clan—plus a heap
of trade goods—in and out of town,
in case the danged ol' truck broke down.

Sometimes he earned a buck or two
by diggin' graves with the city crew,
and one day saw out in the shed
an old hearse. "Jest the thing," he said.

Kids whooped and hollered, "Awesome sight.
Lots of space to feud and fight.
We don't need no padded seat—
we'll perch on sacks of corn or wheat."

That summer temperatures climbed high.
About the middle of July
old Abe's sow, Big Belle, got sick—
and kicked the bucket—mighty quick!

Abe pondered just what he should do.
'Twould take a heap of diggin' to
inter six hundred pounds of meat
in eighty-five degrees of heat.
Besides, the old girl couldn't stay
out in the yard for more'n a day,
because fresh pork don't smell so nice
par-boiled by sun and spiced with lice.

The land-fill would no way allow
a solid mass of stinking sow.
"A grave is what we need," thought he.
"And I know where one's dug for me."

Well, then the pick-up wouldn't start.
In fact, it durn near fell apart.
"With tires flat and battery dead,
we'll have to use the hearse," he said.

Abe called his offspring to his side,
and moaned, "Now, since Big Belle has died,

71

it's only fittin' seems to me,
that we should treat with dignity
one whose life has served us good.
We'll honor her like family should."

They wrapped her bulk in tarp of gray.
Then each one with a big bouquet
of hollyhocks and baby's breath
adorned the hearse for one in death.

They flung the big doors open wide,
and then with four kids to a side,
they heaved and pushed with groan and grunt—
and shoved the carcass toward the front.

They climbed aboard in single file,
and sat like mourners—proper style.
And as it seemed the thing to do,
they started on a hymn or two.

Town folk, hearing mournful strains
of funeral songs, joined in refrains.
Poor Myrt's gone, they would assume,
bedazzled by the mass of bloom.
And though they thought it overdone,
the caravan grew one by one.

Abe, looking neither left nor right,
drove to the graveyard and the site,
backed the hearse up to the pit—
And bent his head to rest a bit.

72

When he got out to dump the sow,
he scratched his head and wondered how
this congregation came to be,
with hats removed respectfully.
But, giving all a puzzled smirk
yanked open rear doors with a jerk.

When eight wild kids came tumbling out
and with abandon ran about,
and odor of the dead arose—
and every mourner held his nose!

Abe helped his ragtag boys to shoo
the flies that round the gray tarp flew,
then with the aid of prod and pole
they plopped the body in the hole.

Jane Smith fainted dead away.
Most turned shades of green or gray.
But Mattie Wilson screamed aloud,
and could be heard above the crowd
by yelling out, "This is no way
to put poor Myrt to rest today!"

Then Abe grinned wide and said, "Well, hell,
That ain't my wife! It's jest Big Belle."

# JIM ROSS

*Jim Ross was born and raised on a ranch in the Bull Mountains of Mus-selshell County, Montana. After five years in the infantry during World War II, Ross returned to Montana where he went into a variety of enterprises, including ranching and a job with the Department of Agriculture. He has published three books of poems,* Get Down and Come In, Pull Up a Chair, *and* Saddle Up and Ride.

## COMMUNICATION

It's morning in the breakfast nook
Of our house on Pine Draw Way.
"Good morning," to my wife says I.
When she answers it's to say:
"Like some porridge or an egg?"
I answer: "That's okay."
I asked her if she read the ad
Of the auction sale today.
She responded with a flurry
And a grapefruit passed my way.
I said: "Sale is called for ten o'clock,
But with the sky so gray
I wonder if the crowd will form
or if they'll stay away."

She mentioned something 'bout a sale,
I hardly caught a word.
I said that we could go right now
and be that early bird.
She said: "Our daughter I must call,
then do a deacon's chore.
If you weren't busy you could help,
there's this to do and more."
She gets her coat, I get my hat.
We exit to the car.
Thinks I, we're going to the auction.
Thinks she, we'll work the church bazaar.
When I noticed I was wrong
Was when she passed the auction gate.
I mumbled 'neath my breath to her:
"Yeah, we communicate?"

# THE POMMEL SLICKER

Some call it just a slicker,
    It's a raincoat to a few;
It's made of stuff called fishskin,
    And it sure keeps out the dew.

It checks those old north breezes,
    The rains don't penetrate;
When its designer changed his grazing.
    He found, to heaven, wide the gate.

It is made to cover rider
        As he sits upon his hoss;
It serves as bed tarpaulin
        As he lies upon the moss.

It is good for keeping weather
        Off that faithful saddle gun;
It has hid the "runnin' iron"
        Of a cattle rustling one.

It's been used as sack for soogans
        And the makins of a stew;
It has graced the rear of cantles
        Since the days of Teddy Blue.

A slicker, like a saddle,
        At any time of year;
And boots and chaps and bedroll,
        Are essential cowboy gear.

Regardless of the season,
        Trail time or time to calve;
It's a yellow pommel slicker
        That you dang well better have.

If a hombre should approach you
        For a job of cowboy kind,
Check his old Al Fursnow*
        For a slicker tied behind.

*Early day saddle made in Miles City, Montana.

If that yellow pommel slicker
    Ain't there in any weather,
The callous on his backside
    Was not made by saddle leather.

If you're looking for a wrangler
    And "Tex" says he meets the creed,
Ask him how he's fitted
    With the gear the job will need.

If he hasn't got a slicker
    Of the yellow pommel kind.
A saddle west of North Platte
    Hasn't cradled his behind.

You've just took on a cowboy
    And he's shivering in the cold,
In a shorty denim jacket
    Nigh his belly button fold.

If he doesn't view a slicker
    As essential as his beans,
Then it wasn't saddle oil
    That stained his Levi jeans.

If you've a hunch that bragging cowboy
    Is made of drugstore stuff,
Ask some pertinent questions,
    Be not afraid to call his bluff.

If a yellow pommel slicker,
    In his gear, is not about,
Then the B.S. on his boots
    Is inside instead of out.

# ANGORA WOOLY CHAPS

Oh, you relics of the past,
    Nobody wears you anymore;
But your place in western archives
    Is richly laced with cowboy lore.

You were practical and comely,
    Served with distinction and a flair;
You were tuxedos in the bunkhouse,
    You old chaps with wooly hair.

A cowboy dressed in woolies
    Just somehow stole the show,
In the moonlight or the sunshine
    He took on a radiant glow.

No, nothing drew attention
    To a cowboy mounted there,
Riding circle or parading,
    As much as chaps with wooly hair.

You weren't just pomp and glitter,
    Though your looks might so portray;

You were worn in self-defense
        Against the hazards of the day.

When in a blinding snowstorm,
        Or 'mong the din of thunderclaps,
You were assuring with your warmth,
        You old angora wooly chaps.

You have wallowed in corral dung,
        Smelled the singe of hair and hide;
You have clung to saddle leather
        On many an outlaw ride.

You have heard the tales of cowboys,
        Some were tall and rank and rare;
Too bad you can't repeat them,
        You old chaps with wooly hair.

Regardless of your color,
        Red or brown or black or white,
You and owner struck a kinship,
        You were essential day or night.

Cowpunching lost some romance
        When barbwire fenced the gaps,
And cowboys lost some luster
        When they quit wearing wooly chaps.

Until all those old-time cowboys
        Take their final starlit naps,

You'll be remembered with affection
    As just plain old wooly chaps.

When that roll is called in heaven
    There will be cowboys there, perhaps;
They'll be swapping mounts and saddles
    But seldom ever wooly chaps.

# ROD NELSON

*R od Nelson ranches with his wife, Teri, near Almont, North Dakota. He is
also a part-time brand inspector, horse trainer, and occasional rodeo per-
former. Nelson has recited his lighthearted verse across Canada and the United
States, as well as on NBC's Tonight Show.*

## PRAIRIE POLITICAL POTENTIAL

When the world situation is unstable
And my heart is filled with fear
I look forward to the comfort
That's found in election year.

When my faith in mankind wavers
And the future looks real bad
I just grab a daily paper
And read a campaign ad.

We're not runnin' short of talent.
There's a surplus to be sure.
The world could create no problems
That these folks couldn't cure.

Qualified? You can bet your boots,
They're that and honest too,

81

The cream that's risin' to the top,
The pride of the red, white, and blue.

Common sense, integrity,
Are virtues I see a lot.
Hard working, experienced leaders,
Folks who can't be bought.

Common, family-loving patriots
Are among those making bids
And even all the bachelor hopefuls
Claim to love their kids.

They're not in it for self-interest,
There's a cross they want to bear.
At serving all of mankind
They just want to do their share.

And as far as all the campaign ads,
Well, I believe them, yes I do.
There's laws for truth in advertising
So I know they must be true.

But I feel a sort of sadness.
It could make a fellow sob.
When the election is finally over
Only half will have a job.

But harken all ye unsuccessfuls,
There's good news to be sure.

Come to western North Dakota
Where there's political jobs galore.

Here opportunity awaits you.
We need those able skills.
Most places have less people
Than positions to be filled.

Folks attend those annual meetings
Not with hopes of being selected,
But if you're not there to defend yourself
You're bound to get elected!

Yes, more offices than people is a problem in our parts,
Too many jobs for everyone, it seems.
If we had a buck for every board there is, and each
committee too, we'd be rich beyond our wildest dreams.

If you're new in our community,
Now you maybe think I'm daft,
But every able-minded
Has to sign up for the civil draft.

You're bound to get some duties,
And just to prove I'm right,
I know of one, new Southern Baptist
Who's been serving as a Knight!

You're cruising for a beating
If you try to hide and skip a meeting

'cause they know everywhere
There is to search.

And you may not have to listen,
But they'll darn sure know you're missin'
If you're not there
Sunday morning in your church.

Raleigh Saddle club's Larry Vetter
Thought his chances would be better
If he could convince
The other members he's unfit.

So he made up a story, his method sure was sorry,
He lied, and not a little bit.
The sly and sneaky vandal
Claimed he'd been in a sex scandal.

But his deception wasn't worth a lousy cent.
His story they weren't buyin'
'cause they knew that he was lyin'
And they elected poor old Larry president.

Well, let's say you are a professional with jobs to delegate,
That's when this situation starts to rub.
You'll know just where to start, and who will do their part,
You may be the only member in the club.

You can get some wild assignments
If they spot you in a meeting.

I heard of one old priest near Amidon
Who teaches classes in breast feeding.

It's hard to get your work done with all those civic chores
And your mind and body seem to be at risk.
You may start out your day with dreams of hauling hay,
By night they'll have you serving Lutefisk.

I know a guy named Dan who tries farmin' when he can,
His extra jobs don't earn this chap a dime.
It seems he's spent half of his life explaining to his wife
Why he's riding with the posse all the time.

And at the Sim's ELCA Christmas program,
Now hang on to your lids,
We've been runnin' short of Lutherans
So we borrow Catholic kids!

And I even heard a rumor,
Now this one's got to be a plug,
Some town, supposedly, has a German-Russian officer
In their Son's of Norway Club.

You'll come under heavy fire, if you ever do retire
And folks think you'll have some leisure time ahead.
The simple fact of it is that most ranchers dare not quit
And keep punching cows until the day they're dead.

This I hate to talk about, but there's only one way out,
Though some organizations can be a little firm.

There was one old boy who died,
Well, just to fix his hide, they stuck him with another term.

If it's experience you need, then my advice you'll heed
And come west to the greatest proving ground.
You may think it's a joke, but when some folks finally croak
Their obituaries weigh at least a pound.

So to make your chances best, migrate to the West
And answer civic duty's call.
You'll darn sure win a race if you dare to show your face,
And we'll get you folks elected one and all.

# DAKOTA FRESH AIR

Those folks down at the tourism department
Sure go through some pains
To brag up and glorify
My state up on the plains.

I saw an ad not long ago
That really did impress me—
Who would have guessed—my state is best
For things one wants to see.

Yes, the pretty photos stunned me.
I would have never thought
I was living in the middle
Of one grand vacation spot.

It stressed our scenic beauty,
Talked up our industry,
Pointed out historic sites
With good ac–cur–a–cy.

They may have praised our weather
A little to Excess
But when they spoke of clean, fresh air—
Well, folks, that's no B.S.

Yes, fresh air is abundant.
It's never stale or sour.
We import the stuff from Canada
At ninety miles per hour.

Air that we are breathing
When it's pretty close to noon
Was probably at breakfast time
Somewhere near Saskatoon.

It's truly quite a blessing
But sometimes it's a sin
When it's traveling by so doggone fast
That one can't breathe it in.

It comes from all directions
But the north winds are the best
The air gets sort of thick sometimes
When the wind is from the West.

I hate these blasted droughty years
Like the ones we've had of late.
A hard west wind is often filled
With Montana real-estate.

But it sometimes works out dandy.
We all thought it was fine,
How we got the Killdeer Mountains
When they blew across the line.

When North Dakota parents
Send their children out to play
They fill their pockets up with rocks
So they won't blow away.

But, by gosh, I'm not complaining,
Though the wind is sometimes mean.
The air that we are breathing
Is truly fresh and clean.

And our weather, oh, it's grand sometimes,
Be it warm or winter chill,
But a good day in North Dakota
Is when that fresh air is standing still.

# MICKY'S MASH

There's something I enjoy since I was a boy,
To me it's a special treat…
Better than fishin', huntin', or just plain relaxin',
It's the feel of new boots on my feet.

But my wife's refrain is that I am just vain,
The pair that I have is O.K.
But dear, it's hard to find pleasure in most any measure
When you wear a size 12 double A.

Funny ideas she has—she'd rather buy food for the kids,
Or rugs for the floors,
So I pulled on my old Tony Lamas
And went out to do up my chores.

I guess I'd say they felt worse that day
Than they had in quite a long while.
One boot was too loose, the other too tight,
My mood changed from ugly to vile.

The tight boot, you see, made no sense to me,
My sock must be all wadded up.
Well, I wouldn't fix it out here in the snow
I'd wait 'till I went in for a cup.

I jerked it off at coffee time
And on a chair did sit.

I saw to my amazement
My big toe was soppin' wet.

As I jerked off the sock, the sight caused a shock.
My heart beat with a thud.
My favorite big toe was not wet from the snow,
It was icky and sticky from blood.

I was checking it out when I heard a shout
From my four-year-old son by the door.
Excited he was, he was pointing at the crushed
And mangled carcass of a mouse upon the floor.

So the mystery was solved as to the blood,
But just how did poor Micky expire...
Was he mashed by my foot, or did he die from the fumes
As he crawled down inside to retire.

Now there was good came from this—Said my Missus
"Those old boots do show some wear.
Throw them right out, 'cause there is no doubt
It's time that you buy a new pair."

# IAN TYSON

*N*o *writer of verse or song has brought the spirit of life on the Northern Range to more people than Ian Tyson. In addition to his busy career as a song writer and performer, Tyson lives on a ranch near Longview, Alberta, where he raises cutting horses. His many record albums include* Old Corrals & Sagebrush, I Outgrew the Wagon, *and* Cowboyography, *from which "Springtime" is taken.*

## SPRINGTIME

Bald eagles back in the cottonwood
tree
The old brown hills are just about
bare
Springtime sighing all along the creek
Magpies ganging up everywhere
Sun shines warm on the eastern slope
March came in like a lamb for a
change
Gary's pulling calves at the old
stampede
We made it through another on the
northern range
Lonnie's pulling calves at the top of

the world
We made it through another on the
northern range
Well the big chinook blew in last
week
Warm and strong from the western
sea
Pretty soon water running
everywhere
Hell it couldn't run fast enough for
me
Broodmare's sleeping in the
afternoon sun
She's shedding hair everywhere
Time for a change
George's pulling calves at the T-Y
We made it through another on the northern range
Waddie's pulling calves at the Little E
We made it through another on the northern range

Bald eagles back in the cottonwood
tree
The old brown hills are just about
bare
Springtime sighing all along the creek
Magpies ganging up everywhere
Sun shines warm on the eastern
slope
March came in like a lamb for a change
Larry's pulling calves at the Quarter
Circle S

We made it through another on the
northern range
Allan's pulling calves at the Bar 4
Oarlock
We made it through another on the
northern range
Jean's pulling calves at the
Horseshoe Bar
We made it through another on the
northern range
Ian's in the hills trying to write songs
Gid's in the country where the tall
grass grows

© KURT HAFSO '92

# ARTHUR PEAKE

*A*rthur Peake was born in Monmouthshire, England, in 1866 and came to Western Canada in 1884. After ranching in the foothills southwest of Calgary, he moved, in 1897, to a larger ranch in the open range country along the Red Deer River—near the present town of Dorothy. Although Peake died in 1947, the ranch is still operated by members of his family. A book of Peake's poems, Ballads from the Badlands, was published by Coyote Books in 1991.

## THE STRAWBERRY ROAN

Come all you old buckaroos and listen to my rhyme
    About the ol' bronc rider that didn't have a dime.
How he tried to ride a pony, and tried to ride him fair,
    And found himself a-sitting on nothing in the air.
For I would like to tell you this rider of renown
    Was born and bred a cowboy and did not live in town.
He was raised way down in Texas and rode the Chisholm Trail
    And all his life had followed up the old cow trail.

About the old roan pony this feller couldn't ride;
    Well no one ever rode him, tho' several of them tried.
He went wild up in the mountains and the cowboys called him Chief;
    So they named a mountain after him, and that is my belief.
All around the campfires they talked of the Strawberry Roan

Who never joined a bunch again but always ranged alone.
They say he fought a puma once and chased him to his lair,
And it wouldn't have surprised me if he'd killed a grizzly bear.

The Indians in the lodges too, still speak of him by name;
For after trailing him for days they could not win the game.
Many wild horse hunters who thought he'd come up short
Just saw a flash of the Strawberry Roan and heard his fearful snort.
He made for the big tall timber and travelled far and wide:
He wintered with the deer and moose and knew just where to hide.

# 1915—GONE ARE THE DAYS

Gone are the days when I was young and gay
Forgotten are the songs I sang upon my way
As I followed up the cattle or crossed the lonely plain
And many a thing that joy did bring I'll never see again.

"They're coming, they're coming," the boys they said to me,
"They'll plow the land all 'round you, and a farmer you will be."

I used to ride a saddle that had a wooden horn
And many a horse I broke to ride before you boys were born.
We handled all beef cattle then like we were shipping eggs
But now they want to get to town so run them off their legs.

"They're coming, they're coming," the boys they said to me,
"They'll plow the land all 'round you, and a farmer you will be."

When we were trailing cattle we'd string them out in file
      But now they have them in a bunch—I do not like their style.
I know that times have changed, both cows and cowboys too,
      And soon they'll haze them in on foot like Eastern drovers do.

They're coming, they're coming, the farmers I do see;
With all the grass turned upside down, where will the grazing be?

Gone are the cattle from off the Bullpound Range,
      Gone is the dipping vat we built to cure the mange.
The settlers through the country think that farming can't be beat
      For there came a good wet season and they raised a crop of wheat.

It's coming, it's coming, dry weather they will see
And if it lasts for many years, where will the farmers be?

# THE OLD TIMER

The sun was sinking in the west,
      the wind for once was still,
As an ancient prairie schooner,
      came roughlocked down the hill.
The driver wore a buckskin coat,
      his pardner's skirts were long,
And as he took his roughlock off
      he sang his favorite song—
We're going West! We're going West!
      We're going to make a home.
We'll settle down forever soon,

and never more will roam.
They camped beside the farmer's fence,
 there were no ranchers now,
For the grass was long ago destroyed
 by the farmer and his plow.
They hobbled out their horses
 in the public right of way,
Then pitched a tent and lit a fire,
 and sang this roundelay—
We're going West! We're going West!
 We're going to make a home.
We'll settle down forever soon,
 and never more will roam.

The farmer's people crowded out
 to see this curious sight,
And listened to the old man's yarns,
 away into the night.
How once he'd worked upon a farm,
 up north near Edmonton.
When one time came the farmer said
 just take this chief my son;
And put him on a rabbit track,
 as sure as I'm a sinner,
And told him then to follow that
 and he would find his dinner.

And then he spoke of Fort MacLeod,
 where the wind doth never stop.
They planted all potatoes there

with a big flat stone on top.
He told about fat bacon sides,
        and said it was a sin—
Condemned for food across the line,
        the freighters brought it in;
And where they stuck a mudhole,
        laid it underneath the wheels.
Then we'd bacon, mixed with syrup,
        and flap-jacks for our meals.

Did you hear about the rancher,
        trailing south from Calgary,
Who used to pick up useful things
        that on the trail he'd see?
Tom said he took a mower, and
        took it bit by bit;
When the foreman said it was his own
        the cowboys took a fit.
He passed a load of lumber once
        that in the mud was stuck,
And took away the double-trees,
        and said, "Well this is luck."
The load was for this rancher,
        and very late that night
The teamster came, right on the prod,
        and looking for a fight.
He'd taken out an extra team,
        and when he came upon
The place he left this wagon,
        why the double-trees were gone.

He talked about Alberta,
        and things that used to be;
And how in all that province
        there were liars only three.
The first one was the rancher
        just mentioned unto you.
An old-timer up near Morley,
        he was the other two.
Once he went to cross a lake
        and Oh! the ice was thin;
He had to go most carefully,
        for fear he would fall in.
He looked around and saw, my friends,
        a sight you won't believe—
The big lake-trout had seen
        the red upon his moccasin.
So he cursed the Stony Indians,
        and to run he did begin;
And as he jumped upon the shore
        the ice it broke for fair,
And a couple of the biggest ones,
        jumped up into the air.
Then one of them fell on a rock,
        as dead as it could be,
And the Stonies snaked it into camp
        and held a jamboree.

Then prohibition stories came;
        way back in '85
The people of Alberta then,

was very much alive.
They got their whiskey in by train,
 and also by the trail,
In Coal Oil Cans, a case of eggs,
 and China marked as "Frail;"
A barrel labeled "Vinegar,"
 was one day found and seized;
A policeman sat on top of it,
 most important, if you please,
Waiting on the platform,
 for an officer to come,
While underneath a genius
 with an augur bored for rum.

When daylight came they went to move
 the barrel for to spill it.
And the Sergeant with a pint flask
 had not enough to fill it.

The night was dark and getting cold,
 the folks began to tire,
And as they wandered home they thought
 he was another liar.
The lady at the wagon said,
 "Well, Bill, you did it grand;
But that sorry bunch of pilgrims
 don't really understand."
We're going West! We're going West!
 across the last divide.
Let's hope we'll find old times there,
 up on the other side.

**100**

# HOME

It's years ago since first I crossed Red Deer
        And roughlocked down those broken banks of clay,
And built my home of cottonwood and willow
        And hauled supplies from Gleichen far away.
The antelope then bunched upon the prairie
        And prairie chicks in thousands we did see,
And with haystacks in our yards when it came winter
        The old Red Deer just looked like home to me.

Our cattle ranged from Willow Creek to Bullpound;
        The open range was good and free to all.
We branded calves, cut hay and then the beef herd
        Was gathered up for shipping in the fall.
A rider then he headed for our rancho
        Says, "A welcome there and feed for horse and me."
We talked on brands, bits and spurs and saddles,
        And the old Red Deer just felt like home to me.

Now it's lonesome today beside the old Red Deer;
        The riders they no longer come this way.
The range is fenced and cut up into homesteads,
        For years we have not even talked of hay.
Beside the Red Deer's banks I have to linger,
        Tho' the future here does not shine bright for me.
Could we hit the trail again for open country?
        For freedom and feed, how happy we would be.

# CHARLIE MILLAR

*Charlie Millar was an Illinois farm boy who followed his brother, Herb, to work in the open range country of southern Alberta in the 1880s. The Millars worked for the North West Cattle Company on the Bar U Ranch when George Lane moved north from Montana to become the Bar U foreman under ranch manager Fred Stimson. Later, Lane began ranching on his own. Then, in 1902, when Millar wrote the following poem for the* Calgary Eye-Opener, *Lane took over the Bar U and forced Stimson out. Recently, the Canadian government designated the Bar U a national historic site.*

## ON THE SALE OF THE BAR U

The shades of night were falling fast
And the Bar U ranch was reached at last
For the YT boss had a telegram
That knocked from the roost the great I Am
Who said "Goddimit!"

The great I Am did cry and moan
So he lifted his foot and kicked a stone
And dear little somebody made an awful fuss
When she left the ranch with the poor old cuss
Who always said "Goddimit!"

It lifted a load from the cowboy's heart
When they saw the old fellow ready to start,
For he docked their wages on a stormy day,
And when they kicked you would hear him say
"Goddimit!"

The Nitchies will miss their bread and jam
Since's they lost their friend the great I Am,
For he's gone to the East perhaps to stay,
And no more the cowboys will hear him say
"Goddimit!"

The great I Am is now no more
And old George Lane will take the floor,
He'll tell the cowboys what to do,
And shake them up with a
"Goddamyou!"

# JIM GREEN

*J*im Green, *an award winning poet who was raised in Pincher Creek, Alberta, has written two collections of verse,* North Book *and* Beyond Here. *He is currently working on a novel.* "Hired Guns" *has recently appeared in* Dry Crik Review, *and* "Wild Card on the North Fork" *has appeared in* White Clouds Review.

## DEAD HORSE WINTER

He made it back to the ranch
in two long days, snow piled
three feet when he left town,
covered the top wires
by dawn next morning
as he leap-frogged along
with two fagged-out horses
lunging at chest deep drifts.

The cattle were bawling
bunched up in the creek bed,
sucked them out with the smell
of loose hay and a trail
punched through by Clydesdales
dragging the sled. He set out

next day for the horses
but his mounts bogged down
just short of the ridge.
He stuck his saddle in a tree
sent the horses on the backtrail
and floundered on alone
with snowshoes made of aspen,
strips from a gray blanket
and strings from the saddle.

The last days were the worst,
searching the still canyons
for stranded wasted bands,
the killing    blood
splattered dark on crystal white,
the numbing slam of the rifle
and the screams.
The lucky ones were dead
already, the rest almost gone,
slumped walleyed in soft snow
just slack hide and hard bones,
they had no tails left and
even manes were missing where
they'd chewed on each other.
Sticks poked through
slashed cheeks, gums raw
bloodied from crushing branches,
the last of the feed.
He shot and kept shooting,
killed a hundred and more

first with a long gun
till he ran out of shells,
finishing the last of them off
with an old Savage shotgun.

In the spring a gelding
with eight gaunt mares in tow
came down from the valley,
survived the snow.

# HIRED GUNS

All night long they lay
forted on the bale stack
wrapped in parkas and robes
against the driving snow,
the icey midnight winds.

Waiting with covered guns
eyes knifing the black
and flying flakes
of February winter,
sipping thermos coffee,
wishing they were home.

Finally      the elk came,
gaunt shadows in the blur
they trod cautiously
hooves cracking the crust
stopping      listening

```
    starving     advancing
driven from the mountains
hunger     overcoming fear
    closer
            closer
                then wheeling
        away in terror
racing from gun thunder,
splash of pluming rifles.


Climbing down off the stack
stiff     smell of cordite,
cold     sounds of running
the wind     and tomorrow
more of the same     saving
the hay     for the cattle.
```

# WILD CARD ON THE NORTH FORK

It happened sometime before 1910. Winter.

Over at Allan Kennington's place on the North Fork.
Three of them ole boys was whooping it up a tad.
Kennington's neighbor name of Stepney was there,
and Jimmy Milvain had rode over from his place on
Cow Creek. Enjoying some cards and passing a jug
around they were.

While they was waiting for Stepney to decide if he
wanted to be hit or not they heard a soft but solid

**107**

thud in the bedroom. Kennington took the lamp off
the table and opened the door a crack. He spotted
a young mountain lion on the bed. He closed the door
real quiet like and the three of'm got organized.

Stepney whipped the door open. Milvain pushed the
lamp in the bedroom. Kennington squeezed off a shot.
Stepney slammed the door shut, trapping Milvain's
arm in the bedroom with the lamp and the lion.
Kennington shouldered the door open. Milvain
reunited himself with his arm and while the door
was wide open, they all took a look-see.

Milvain lugged the cougar out to the woodshed.
Kennington changed the counterpane on the bed.
There was no aces or faces showing. Stepney had
a four up, five and jack down. He stayed with
nineteen.

# THE KID WITH THE CUT-AWAY HOLSTER

The bullet entered his leg
just below the tied-down
cut-away fast draw rig,
there was a straight red line
running to about the knee
and a wandering blue track
to where the Doc dug it out
just above the top
of his Acme Western boot.

108

# THELMA POIRIER

*T**helma Poirier ranches near Fir Mountain, in southwestern Saskatchewan. Her poetry has been widely anthologized, as well as published in* Double Visions, *a book co-authored with Jean Hillabold, and* Grasslands, *from which the following poems are taken.*

## AT THE BRANDING

years ago
women were never allowed
to go to the branding

their daughters move with ease
across the corral
one of them picks up grandpa's knife
holds it firmly in one hand
in the other she clutches the pouch
full and soft like a chamois purse

snip     slice
the bottom falls from the purse
blood like copper pennies
stains the calf's white leg

her fingers press the flesh

bring down the larger coins

the blade again

she dips the knife in antiseptic
is ready for the next calf

forty steers later
she leaves the corral
the knife folded in her pocket

# ONE TEXAS COWBOY

he was a boy
when he left Texas
a man by the time
the herd trailed
into Canada

along the trail
sometimes trigger happy
sometimes shy
quick with cards
he knew when to let them die

always down and out
never quite broke
before his mother died
she gave him a Bible

cows
he knew cows
could tell you about each one
each cow in a herd of thousands
some mark, a tick of white
a small blue roan
some errant behavior
the ones that pawed
the ones that charged

when he died
friends lowered him into the ground
they say an old cow
hung her head on the fence and bawled

*

women, ah the women
he used to say
fingered a pearl-handled six gun

we hear the legends
how he maybe shot a man
defending a lady's honor
in a saloon across the line
how it happened
years before he settled on Rice Creek

he never married
but sometimes in the sun's last warmth
he would say the words once or twice
the women, ah the women
and the way he spoke
set mosquitoes humming

*

we went to see the holes in the floor
the bullet holes, evidence
left from a game of five card stud
played without honour

we found ashes
settled in the stone foundation
walked around
wondering if anything we came across
once belonged to him

if the boot, dry as cow dung
shrinking on the prairie once fit smooth
over his ankle

if the coil of rusted wire, the willow pickets
rotting were part of a fence he built
part of his horse pasture

# THE GRUBLINE

from ranch to ranch
Jack Henderson rode the grubline
it was always howdy and come in
we were just sitting down for dinner
pull up a chair

Jack ate enough for three hired men
hoped the missus didn't mind if he had another smoke
while she went out and milked the cow

and in the winter it was Jack
spreading butter pale as lard
over a plate of pancakes
Jack, saying what a fine cook the missus was
how he'd be glad to pull up to her table anytime

we heard it all before

*

winter and the hermits popped out of the hills
three days before Christmas
one by one they crowded the beds
rolled boys onto quilts on the floor

they worked for their board, chopped wood
kept fires burning

113

sometimes rocked the baby in the afternoon
warmed their feet in the oven

much like badgers
when spring came they disappeared
left behind great big holes

# SHEEPHERDERS

sheepherders spent the winter in Moose Jaw
or Gravelbourg
holed up in second rate hotels

upright Scots, errant French men
you never asked them any questions
they could not answer with their eyes

one herder, old
old I suppose because he had a beard
sat on the end of the bench
smoked in my mother's kitchen
taught me to light matches
one day herding sheep, the next day fired

summer passed slowly in a sheep camp
sheep wagon on a knoll
a creek nearby
a hillside where sheep lay warm
beneath their breath at night

coyotes never far away
sheepdog growling

sheepherders sometimes men
sometimes boys
slept with a gun beside them

herding sheep, they dreamed winter nights in town
in town, they dreamed sheep

# COLONEL SCHEETZ, FOREMAN OF THE N-N

we just kept shoving those cows north
before long they were moving on their own
wandering up creeks
drifting with the heat to the headwaters
of Rock Creek, the west Poplar
we followed with a string of saddlehorses
chuckwagons

Neidringhaus took out a lease
a cent an acre for a hundred thousand acres
that's how the N–N came to Canada

summer when we came, then winter
the winter of eighty-six
a tough winter
those Mounties at the Post could tell you

half the herd     six thousand head
became skeletons in the willows

we pulled south
set up camp along the Missouri
before long our cattle wandered up the creeks again
we used the open range
without a lease

# NEIL MEILI

*Neil Meili grew up on a ranch on the north shore of Old Wives Lake in southern Saskatchewan. Since then, his business activities have included ranching, real estate, scriptwriting, and film production. He divides his time between Calgary, Alberta, and Austin, Texas.*

## ROUND UP

It's about the hardest dustiest best work a man can get.

The pride of the heeling rope, thrown snake quick from a good horse and the slow steady pull; dragging the white face out where the boys with the hot irons can record the feat.

Three hundred cows sing of calves lost and found, and above and through it all the full strong laugh of one of the boys, where a slip was made or a kick well placed.

At the end of the day; you wrap a rope-sore hand around a spring-cold beer, and lean back against the old pole fence; deep in the pain, and the sweat, and the moment.

completely released from the wheel of desire

117

there's no place you'd rather be

there's no one you'd rather be with

and you're too damned tired to move anyway

# PRAIRIE CHICKEN

I came up through the valley where the homesteaders had tried to make a go of it for a few years, past the tin cans and other evidence of their short stay trying to rust itself back into the ground. Up over the crest of the hill where the Indians had lived for centuries with no more evidence than some of nature's favorite shapes.

It was spring and I stumbled onto what they may have seen for years, the ageless mating ceremony of about twenty five or thirty grouse. They didn't see or hear me and I stopped about ten yards away and watched, although my mother might not have thought it proper.

The hens ran around, heads down and tails high in unbashful invitation, while the cocks puffed up the air bags in their chests and drummed their challenge.

And they looked handsome and brave in their posturing and beckoning and their readiness for reckoning. And the fights were on, straight on and straight up, with spurs and feathers flying.

It was vicious but pure. Not a cock fight for the amusement of the bloody-minded, but a way to see that only the strongest would sire the little broods that would have to survive the hawks and the snakes and the weather, and all the dangers of a land where it takes a great deal of courage—just to be a chicken.

# THE LONELY MEN

Their little dark houses still dotted the prairie
when I was growing up.

They all seemed to cling to the soil as if their life-force had
all been used up in the long and difficult transplanting
and they could hang on but no longer grow.

Or they stood alone surrounded by sadness and the small and
smaller markers of what had fallen
to the reaper's scythe.

Their roots loosened year after year by the hot winds and the
deep frosts; they became more and more brittle
until one by one they broke off
like tumbleweeds
                    and were gone.

# HARVEY MAWSON

*H*arvey Mawson's great-grandfather established one of Saskatchewan's first cattle ranches in 1881. Since then, there have been six generations of the Mawson family on the land. Although Mawson has recently retired from ranching, he continues to write about the life of ranchers and cowboys. In addition to his book of short stories, Cowboy Up, *Mawson has published two books of verse*, Brimstone & Bobwire *and* Truth, Legends, & Lies. *He is currently working on a novel.*

## A FIVE DOLLAR CATTLE DRIVE

If cattle ride in liners
  it saves on wear and tear,
beats hell out of trailin' cows
  t' git from here t' there.
Not harpin' on the subject,
  but it seems not long ago
when our ways by present standards
  would be judged a might too slow.

Like when old Mike moved his cows
  in the spring of forty-five,
bein' lured by extra cash
  I was hired for the drive.
It took a half day's ridin'

just t' git me there,
done of course on my time;
         We agreed that this was fair.


The herd was corralled near midnight
         by a pale moon's feeble light,
cows and calves all bawling,
         shadows driftin' through the night.


Bedded down on the prairie
         where cold wind fingers probe
old Mike snored there beside me
         wrapped up in a horsehide robe.
Sleep for me was intermittent,
         a kid sure feels the cold.
I hoped to grow a thicker skin
         if I lived t' be that old.


Mike rolled out t' light the fire.
         Breakfast was at four.
Sidemeat, bannock, and coffee black
         thawed out my frozen core.
When a draft disturbs his sleep,
         he bantered, a smart man shuts the door.
Fresh air, says I, don't bother me,
         'twas y'r all night honkin' snore.


We lined them out at daybreak,
         and pointed them up the trail.
Hoof, horn, and curly hide
         in a crawling serpent's tail.

The sun came up like fire
       soon warming humpy backs.
At days end its lingerin' flames
       flanked our dusty tracks.

It was after sunset when
       we turned them on the lease.
Six more miles under distant stars,
       and then I'd sleep in peace.
A long day for short pay
       in the spring of forty-five,
earnin' my keep the easy way
       on a five dollar cattle drive.

Being bound by tradition
       this is hard t' say,
but I truly admire the technology
       that helps us all today.
Cattle ridin' liners
       sure as I'm still alive
beats hell out of trailin' cows
       on old Mike's one day drive.

Still I sometimes wonder,
       and I'll leave this up to you;
Who in the end is better off
       when the day is through?
Old Mike had five dollars,
       and he could spare the time.
Now, can we afford a liner
       when the banker owns our dime?

# SID MARTY

*Sid Marty is an Alberta poet and author. His books include* Men For The Mountains *and* Nobody Danced With Miss Rodeo, *from which the following poems are taken.*

## NOBODY DANCED WITH MISS RODEO

And she was too dignified to hula-hula
with the heavy-thighed Hawaiian
dancing girls, entertaining the yokels
in a hockey rink turned beer garden
for Round Up Daze

Nobody danced with Miss Rodeo
in their ersatz Munich cum phony Waikiki
though they rushed the stage to don
fluorescent grass skirts
indulging a Treasure Island fantasy
forgetting the prairie
and its adult pain
free of the wind and the hail
wreathed in exotic leis
of polyurethane
bellies wobbling

the sons and daughters
of the pioneers
of every prairie nationality
had buried their differences
in one dance
the Swedepolukulelewaspgermanic polkahula
It would have thrilled to very jism
the minister of multiculturalism

Too bad he had declined the invite

O Rank Montanon!
Whiskey trading founder
of old Whoop-Up town
deeply buried beneath our pleasure
your skull must be
rattling in this din
like a lusty cash register

Miss Rodeo, demure, was not amused
Few cowboy hats were seen
(bobbing above the crowd
of local merchants)
to rally round the bright
red Stetson of their Queen

Most cowboys had been slightly
crocked up in the afternoon stampede
by bulls and broncs and whatnot
and drinking to ease the pain

124

were in no mood for hula-ing
and foola-ing around a hockey rink
this far east of Waikiki

In the middle of the hot
baldheaded prairie
The only cowboy hats flopped graceless
round the ears of rent-a-cops
descending on a sodbuster, who
undeterred by the grim
aura of fun
let out a rebel "Whoopee!" then
being of Gaelic stock
jumped on a table of beer
to dance the Highland fling
brandishing a jack-knife for a sword

Ah Miss Rodeo
I rose in pity to enquire
but froze, seeing in your eyes

Open range and water rights
Private schools in Switzerland
Sagebrush and contempt

With the image of a paraplegic
Cowboy Prince
crushed by the wing
of a bull named Airtime
a vanquished buckeroo

who's bumpersticker credo was
"I'm a lover, a fighter
and a wild bull rider"

But Miss Rodeo
surely you will recognize
a cowperson?
Peruse these Acme riding boots
elegantly trimmed in dung...

How can you partake, my Queen,
of this Kiwanis fantasy?
Let me chronicle your worth
among the bellowing herd
of homogenized Kanucks

I see your beauty
speechless in polyester
and I appreciate the stallion
parked outside
at the gate of disappearing mountains

So leave with me
and be my *leitmotif,* oh muse!

Miss Rodeo did not deign
to speak, but coolly followed me
out for a little *lebensraum*

Out where the boys were drinking whiskey

126

and quietly licking their wounds
wrapped in their jeans and glory

Old hands tune the fiddle and guitar
A hole in the clouds lets in the prairie stars
Miss Rodeo, their eyes light up
at your approach
"Pull up a beer case, ma'am
and set a spell"

Here are your few
your aching subjects
waiting for you to bless
their scars; waiting for you
to judge their stories

# I'M SO LONESOME IN THE SADDLE SINCE MY HORSE DIED

"Well, he rode the bush rodeos.
He was sure enough a cowboy,
he was a hand.

God he was rank, though!
Always ridin' his horse through some bar,
such a tired old trick.

He done that in Cochrane.
Comes chargin' thru the pickups out front

127

and right through the front door.
And if he wasn't doin' it,
he was holdin' the door
for some other rangy-tang.

One time he rode in with his lariat—
roped guys right outta their chairs
skidded them into the parking lot like calves…

Boy they was hungry for him that day!
All them drugstore cowboys from Calgary,
chased him with trucks all over town
That horse jumpin' fences and
him duckin' clotheslines
with bedsheets and pantyhose
strung around his neck.
That was a pretty tame mount he had
that time, I tell yuh.

They call 'em 'urban cowboys' now,
yuh know. Shee-it!
Buncha drunken half-ton jockeys
all duded up in their Rexall regalia,
they couldn't cut 'im off,
just smashed each other up instead,
at every corner.
He made it to the river
and hid out in the trees.

Ain't it strange
how well some men can ride

yet never make good horsemen.
He treated horses like he hated 'em.

I disremember when it was
he bought this mighty gelding, Boots.
That pony really threw the honkytonk
on Jim, he could not stay aboard.

So he tripped old Boots
with a Scotch hobble.
Yuh know he kept that pony down
until its hooves came near
t' fallin' off.

I always suspicioned him to be
'bout two bricks short of a load
but that was a bit too western for me.

Old Boots was about ruined.
'Fox the sonmuhbitch then,'
says Jim.
'He'll make some dog sick.'
(He didn't like dogs, either)

His wife, though, she was a wonderful woman,
a big skookum girl from Spillamacheen
but a beauty.

Never asked for much, 'cept once.
She wanted a TV. Well, he bought her one
in town, threw it in the truck

and proceeds home, drunk
which was his rule
over Texas gates
at amazin' speeds...

Natchrally the set
got bucked into the tulies...
But he gathered up the remains
and when he got home
dumped this junk on the floor, says
'There's yer TV, hon.
It's a color one, too.'

And he laughed, that fool.
Figured it was a helluva joke.

She never left him, though.
What a woman sees in a man like that,
I'll never know.

Guess he met his Waterloo
in the Caroline Hotel
—some big roughneck dismounted him real hard.
A month of hospital rations kinda tamed him down...

Next I heard, they'd moved to Utah.
Guess he was a bit ashamed of it all.
He was born too late, yuh see,
for the time he was livin'.
Like when we was ropin' cows,
he'd never wear gloves...

He says 'They never wore gloves, the old guys.'
Well jeez you know they couldn't afford 'em, probably!
His hands was like hamburger, but he'd say,
'The only thing yuh can do well with gloves on
is shit yer pants.'

He wouldn't even wrap the horn with rubber
to take the dallies. The old timers never
used that, either. 'Well you dipstick,'
I told him, 'they didn't have it to use, is why.'
All they had was that shaganappi, rawhide.

Then he'd tag some old bitch of a Hereford,
and he'd burn them hands, Lordy!
Make yuh cringe to see it…

Just a big stubborn kid all his days
Livin' in the past
he never knew,
gettin' it wrong all the time.

Maybe that's what it was
with her. Some women love a loser…

Anyway, he was sure enough
aw–thentic cowboy.

He was a hand."

# THERE WAS A LADY MET A BEAR
# (in Jasper National Park)

There was a lady met a bear
The lady, wearing cold cream
Was lying naked in a tent
Beside a mountain stream

This lady had a sunburn, and
I should have said before
How really terrified she was
When the bear came through her door

So quietly, on padded feet
With expression somewhat bored

There must be fats in cold cream
and oils that black bears love
—Someone should do a study
Though I don't know what it'd prove

Perhaps it's high in protein too
—I really do not know
But the black bear licked the lady
In her tent, so cool and shady
The black bear licked the lady
From her head down to her toes

The lady didn't scream, oh no

But, terrified, lay still
Trembling 'neath the black bear's tongue
It was pink and insatiable

And when the black bear ambled off
She dressed, got in her car
And hurried to the nearby town
To buy another jar

# ANDREW SUKNASKI

*A*ndrew Suknaski was born on a homestead near Wood Mountain, in south-western Saskatchewan. His poems have been collected in numerous books and anthologies.

## JAMES LETHBRIDGE

*i love buckin broncos*
*but love women more* he says as he reminisces
about his rodeo days

talks of drinking with pete knight and soak and toata brown
in moose jaw the summer of 1930
and how they were heading west to the calgary stampede
how he wondered whether to return to wood mountain rodeo
or travel west with them

and he says: *now here was my problem*
*am i going to go to calgary buckin broncos*
*or am i going to return to wood mountain and my good woman?*
*this was the predicament i was in*
*now what would you have done?*
*anyway i said to the fullas in moose jaw*
*"i'm goin with a woman in wood mountain*

*and i'm suppose to go back to wood mountain*
*if i don't go back to wood mountain*
*maybe she'll disown me"*

and so he bought a ring and returned home
married the young woman and lived happily for thirty years
and never has seen the calgary stampede
now lives alone in the village
still makes the odd purse or pocket wallet

he spends most of his afternoons in the trails end
drinking calgary beer or whiskey and water
has all the memories he needs here
to sustain him—
arrives nightly at the town well where the children once played
in the playground
slowly pumps a pail of water to make another lonely pot of coffee
and slowly ambles coughing all the way home
carrying something more than merely a pail of water

# THE BITTER WORD

from fort walsh
colonel irvine brings the bitter word
to sitting bull at wood mountain
makes clear the government welcomes the teton—
yet they must not expect provisions
or food from canada

sitting bull proudly replies:
*when did i ever ask you for provisions?*
*before i beg*
*i will cut willows for my young men to use*
*while killing mice to survive*

in the spring of 1881
sitting bull gathers his remaining 1200 sioux
and treks to fort qu'appelle to make
the final request for a reservation—
inspector sam steele tells them
the great white mother wishes them to return
to their own country
(a rather curious view of a people
whose meaning of country changes with
the migrations of tatanka)
steele politely refuses the request
and supplies enough provisions for the return
to wood mountain

death by summer is certain
while irvine makes sure
provisions and seed never arrive

seeing the migrating game
sitting bull knew the tatanka
would never return
though his people dreamed of white tatanka rising
from the subterranean meadows others fled to
(hideous shrieks of red river carts grating in

their ears)
he must have sensed the hunger to follow
which was exactly what the authorities hoped for
on both sides of the border

# THE TETON SIOUX AND 1879 PRAIRIE FIRE

*I consider it impolitic to give Bull a reservation in our country. He is the shrewdest and most intelligent Indian living, has the ambition of Napoleon, and is brave to a fault. He is respected as well as feared by every Indian on the plains. In war he has no equal, in council he is superior to all. Every word said by him carries weight, and is quoted and passed from camp to camp.*

*a letter to the minister of the interior* by major walsh

sitting bull
a legend flowering along the lips
of aboriginal people telling the story
around campfires across the unfenced plains

sitting bull
among the ghosts of my youth
i try to imagine him
the lines around his eyes reminiscent
of shadowed prairie trails in the late afternoon sun
where he sits musing by a lonely campfire
some evening outside the rice valley lodge
in wood mountain—

what did he feel or think
smelling the southern plains burning above the missouri
wood mountain incised by the moving sword of fire
may have looked like a sundancer
beneath heatwaves
the dancing plains fastened by smoke coiling to
the dark orange moon
while he and his people fled to seek refuge
in the wood mountain post

in the police post
major walsh agrees to feed the teton
till bull's two messengers return with news
of the others who journeyed to reservations
near fort buford in the states—
the deceived messengers return with tobacco gifts
and a goodwill missive for the chief
they weave tales of the happy well-fed people
—which the other teton are
for several days anyway
rejoicing over extra rations distributed
before the northern messengers arrive

# NEZ PERCÉS AT WOOD MOUNTAIN

*we came from the earth*
*and our bodies must go back to the earth*
*our mother*

toohoolhoolzote (nez percés prophet)

1

that place where the soul goes
to lie among buried bones
and ancestral dreams
when we leave our boyhood town farms and hills
to journey to the plains—
and they too
the nez percés who survived
to flee up to wood mountain
believed something of this movement
rendering one
faceless

2

heinmot tooyalaket
or better known as young chief joseph
whose father rose to chieftainship in dawn
of nez percés along clearwater river

old chief joseph opening his heart to white men

139

lewis and clark 1805
nez percés feeding the explorers' horses
that summer
while the two men canoe to the pacific

old chief joseph and his people migrating later
to wallowa valley
the new home
green vast meadows
with forests abundant with game—
winding waters and a bluegreen lake

in 1871 the father dies
and chieftainship passes to young son joseph
who shares his father's hospitality
toward white men—
white men later lust for gold in nearby mountains
and finally rustle nez percés' cattle and ponies
(white bird's unheeded warnings
becoming a bitter reality)

gold seekers and politicians twist truth
turning nez percés' honour and name into a jingle—
the truth being
that the gold seekers are the rustlers
and of course
the great father of america gives nez percés
the usual ultimatum:
*move to lapwai reserve or suffer the ensuing fate—*
*the bloodthirsty bluecoats*

3

moccasin telegraph telling of wood mountain
the possible refuge
the peaceful santee dreams and sleep
and the teton sioux (their refuge)

young chief joseph dreams of these through
the uncertain sleep of mountain nights

nez percés
finally moving up through the northwest to
the bearpaw mountains
miraculously battling the bluecoats for a thousand miles—
their chief surrendering one night
while white bird and last followers creep through
a dark coulee beyond bluecoats sentries
(nez percés fleeing north to wood mountain
as chief joseph gives last speech
steeped in abandoned hope
to later die of a broken heart)

4

*i am tired of fighting*
*our chiefs are killed*
*looking glass is dead*
*toohoolhoolzote is dead*
*the old men are all dead*
*it is the young men who say yes or no*
*he who led the young men is dead*

*it is cold and i have no blankets*
*no food*
*no one knows where they are*
*perhaps freezing to death*
*i want time to look for my children*
*and see how many of them i can find*
*maybe i shall find them*
*among the dead*

5

wood mountain
the winter is cold and the game has vanished—
santee and teton children cry: *tacko eena...*

somewhere north of the montana border
the last nez percés are met by sitting bull
walsh and 1000 teton warriors ready for battle
(all are startled by the appearance
of the bedraggled nez percés)

nez percés
death ambling clothed in rags—
children with arms and legs snapped by bullets
wounded children tied and hanging from
the saddle horns
while men and women and horses are nothing
but a walking graveyard

sitting bull and his men befriend the broken people
take them home to lodges

near the old wood mountain post—
nurse them back to health again
and later provide lodges and a place to call home
somewhere to restore something of a dream
a face and pride—
white bird finally affirming some night
before the teton chief and others around a campfire:
*i have no country*
*i have no home and i feel*
*i have no people*

# DORIS BIRCHAM

*D*oris Bircham and her husband ranch in the Cypress Hills near Piapot, Saskatchewan. Her poems and articles have appeared in several magazines and anthologies, as well as on CBC radio.

## HE TELLS IT LIKE IT WAS

over thirty years I bin ranchin' an' I ain't seen nothin' like it before just out ridin' checkin' my herd when I sees this cow tryin' to calve a mean ol' cow she is too an' I see the tips of the calf's feet showin' an' wouldn't you know there's two hind feet you can tell the hind ones 'cause they're upside down but that cow settles right in to pushin' has that calf all by herself even though it's comin' backwards she jumps right up starts mooin' and lickin' an' I'm some relieved so I rides off a hundred yards or so where another cow's gettin' right to it I look 'er over the water bag's just startin' to show she'll be awhile yet and when I ride back to that first cow there she is lying' flat out an' I say sure as hell she must be havin' twins but no she's deader 'n road kill stretched out on the hillside with a chunk of the calf bag hangin' out her mouth you know that slimy skin the calf's born in not the afterbirth hell no just the calf bag so I jumps off my horse I pull on that skin but it breaks right off couldn't have done a damn thing if I'd been right there while she was chokin' the calf's standin' there beside its dead mother just standin' lookin' up at me so I heads for home gets me a bottle an' I milk that dead cow pour that first milk into the calf seems like the best thing I can do for the both of them for now with it so close to bein' dark

**144**

# FORECLOSURE

*it's just dirt,* she said,
that's what I thought when I came to this farm
before I saw the field my husband's grandfather
ploughed with a team of oxen, before I walked
inside teepee rings in the east pasture and drank
from a spring bubbling up from the ground     before
I watched Canada geese come back and nest year after year
along the creek bank and I heard frogs
in our pasture slough announce spring's arrival
and I planted trees

before I learned to ride with my face to the wind
when I hadn't yet smelled new mown alfalfa or seen heads
heavy with wheat bow beneath the sun

it was before I learned about stillborn calves
before I helped feed cattle in a blizzard
and stayed up all night with a heifer
then watched her mother up with her newborn calf

when I'd experienced more seed times than harvests
and watched swaths lay for six weeks
rotting in the rain
and after I'd helped trail cattle to their summer pasture
year after year     gradually I knew
*this is not just dirt, this is our land*

all this happened long before our children

**145**

picked crocuses on the hillside behind our barn
long before we couldn't find the words to tell them
we have to leave

# ON THE MOVE

our neighbor wants to move, anywhere
to get away from these frigid damn winters
he thinks Palliser was right when he said
our triangle is a place unfit
to drag a living from the soil

we've thought that, too
especially when two years of drought
were followed by frosts that killed
and grasshoppers came
to clean up what was left

and the time is now, we said
before our children's shoe laces
are tied to this land

we travelled north to the shelter
of pines where in winter stillness
when smoke spiralled above us
we floundered
in a thick quilt of snow

in the mountains we lingered
by transparent streams

146

breathed the smell of damp cedar
yet we felt strange without sunsets
where rocky peaks draw a curtain
across each day

we moved to Edmonton
walked on carpets and concrete
every day rode on elevators
shoulder to shoulder with people
whose names we never did know

and when we drove where the wheatlands
spread out like a perma-pressed sheet
we were homesick for hills

we came back here where we move cattle
from one field to the next, where
crested wheat usually greens in the spring
heat waves ripple across each summer
and in fall the ditches are goldenrod-lined
in winter when the coulees are bowls
full of shadow there's still a place
for dreams

our neighbor goes south now
for the winter, he says even the geese
have enough sense for that
my husband says, where else
could we feel each season's heartbeat
and where else but here can the wind
fill each empty space

# RAY ANDERSON

*R*ay Anderson has worked on a number of ranches in southern Alberta, including the Bingo and V Bar V. He has now retired to a small ranch on the Red Deer River. "The Longhorn Exodus" is taken from his book, Yarns of a Cowboy.

## THE LONGHORN EXODUS

Ten thousand head of longhorns, strung out across the plains,
Leaving their native Texas, for a far Dakota range.
Thirty days out on the trail, we're shy two thousand head,
From the toll the red man's taken, and the crossing of The Red.

Eight thousand head of longhorns, bedded for a welcome rest,
But the air is full of static, as a storm builds in the west.
The nighthawk's song comes down the wind, as they try to sooth the herd,
All hands are up and saddled, as the ramrod gives the word.
An old bull lunges to his feet, with frightened, rolling eyes,
As thunder rocks the heavens, and lightning streaks the sky.
With slickers buttoned to the throat, we face the lashing rains,
All hell has broken loose tonight, and the devil prowls the plains.
The herd is now up and running, like some angry beast of prey,
And I only hope we all shall live, to see the break of day.
For all that's left 'tween you and death, is your frightened running steed,

And you pray that God will hold your hand, as you ride to bend the lead.
The storm has passed, we've gathered, the cow boss shakes his grizzled head,
We're short a mess of cattle, and a damn good cowboy dead.
On a rise of land we buried Slim, where the grass grew thick and tall,
Just one more Texas cowboy, who won't make it home this fall.

Six thousand head of longhorns, smell water up ahead,
It's the wide Missouri River, and it fills our hearts with dread.
But the trail boss looks it over, and we know he will not sway,
He ropes a handy yearling, spurs his bronc into the spray.
Then we're in there swimming, the water swift and deep,
We wished we'd stayed in Texas, and raised some mangy sheep.

So in the Black Hills of the Dakotas, where the bison once did roam,
Five thousand head of longhorns, have finally made it home.
Of the riders some will settle, no more to risk their neck,
Some will return to Texas, to make yet another trek.

# GLEN RAFUSE

*Glen Rafuse raises Black Angus cattle in the Moutney Valley near Fort St. John, British Columbia, on one of North America's most northerly ranches. He has been writing poems for nearly twenty years.*

## HORSES AND MEN

They were gathered round
The fire one night
These gray-haired
Time-worn men
Just sippin' their beer
And their coffee too
And recallin' those days
"Way back when."

When the Gang Ranch
Ran for a hundred miles
And your summer camp
Was a packhorse load
When fences were made
Of jack pine rails
And the Chilko Ranch
Was the end of the road!

When the saddle you rode
Was center-fire rigged
And your horse
Wore the JH brand
When raisin' good steers
Took two or three years
And hay was stacked
By horses and men!

And the wood that
Fired the big iron stove
Where you fed
Was all split by hand
And the creeks and canals
That watered the fields
Were all built there
By horses and men.

And each man in turn
Spoke of lessons he'd learned
Some remembered the
Blisters and pride
Of ten-hour days
On the haystack
And the creak of that old "beaver-slide!"

No they'd never forget
Old Jimmy Rosette
The craziest breed
On that old JH crew

He was beat-up and lamed
By the broncs he had tamed
And even bears—
Cause he'd roped quite a few!

There were boys who
Drove teams in the summer
And in winter hauled
Feed to the cows
On racks made of wood
Yes, those times were good
And you can bet that
It's all different now!

But around that campfire
There wasn't one liar
These were cowhands
From times "way back when"
As they noted with pride
All those famous "wild rides"
And all the work
Done by horses and men!

# CORKY WILLIAMS

*L*uther *"Corky" Williams grew up in the small ranching town of Van Horn, Texas. In 1971, he moved to British Columbia's west Chilcotin where he ranched until an accident forced him to give up the livestock business. Since then, he has worked as an actor and storyteller. He also appears regularly at cowboy poetry gatherings.*

## THE APRICOT POODLE BOLD

I had bought a ranch in the Canadian West
Up in the B.C. wilds.
I was drawn by the cowboy way of life,
I had loved it since a child.

But here there were bear, near everywhere,
There was moose and deer and fowl
And sometimes at night, just out of sight,
we'd hear the big boy howl.

Well, I soon fell in with some Indian friends
That I met in that big land,
And soon I knew some cowboys, too,
And they extended me their hand.

There was one I met, that I shan't forget,
And he taught me the open range,
Was a cowboy who in '52 had
Moved to this land so strange.

Now, he knew the land like the back of his hand.
He knew every creek and draw,
And he became my good friend, this horseman thin,
And his name was Wild-Man Bob.

Now, a friend of Bob's, for doing a good job,
Had offered him a gift.
Here, choose your dog from this catalog
It'll give your life a lift.

Well, he thought about that, as he pushed his hat,
And pondered on what to choose,
'cause this dog came free, as Bob could see,
And he had nothing to lose.

So, he picked him a dog from the catalog
And waited for him to come.
He had chosen the poodle, a noble breed,
By grabs, this could be fun.

He was shipped from the States, in a little wee crate,
And what waddled out was a sight.
Out come this prize, with weeping eyes,
He would put his own mother to flight.

He walked right out on his little bowlegs

And he shook his bubble head
And we knew right off that a Chihuahua dog
Had slept in his momma's bed.

He was supposed to be pure, but we knew damn sure
This just wasn't the case.
He had little pig ears—he'd panic the steers—
And, good God, what a face.

He had little cross-eyes and knobby knees
And a bit of a crooked jaw.
He was apricot-colored, with a little red ass,
And that, folks, is what we saw.

"If that's a poodle, I'll turn into a noodle,"
I heard the wild man say.
"Good God, Ben, I've been skinned again.
Hell, I'm getting drunk today."

So we broke out the booze—what could we lose—
And we poured out one for the pooch.
To our surprise, right before our eyes,
He lapped up all that hooch.

"Hell, here's a friend, he'll fit right in,"
The wild man said to me.
"Let's teach him to ride, dad-burn their hide,"
And the poodle grinned with glee.

Now, the apricot poodle was a hell of a dog,
And he loved to ride and drink,

And if he didn't get his daily grog,
He'd raise one hell of a stink.

He'd howl and groan and piss and moan
Until we filled his cup.
With his little pink tongue a singing a song,
He'd lap all that whiskey up.

Then he'd give us a smile and sit back a while
And when the whiskey took hold
He'd shake his hide—he was ready to ride—
This Apricot Poodle Bold.

Now, the Apricot Poodle rode standing up
With his front feet on Wild Bob's back.
We built him a saddle, just behind the cantle,
Made out of an old tow sack.

He learned to ride like the wind, with his new-found friends,
Just like a rodeo champ.
But this poodle dog demanded his grog
Whenever we might camp.

We would fix him some chuck and fill up his cup
And throw some more wood on the fire.
Then without a peep, he'd drift off to sleep,
And dream about being a sire.

He dreamed of canine girls, with perfume and curls,
That trot on Vancouver streets.
And he'd give all his pay, this very day,

If one he could really meet.

In the mornings he jumped in the middle of rumps
And rousted us out in the fog.
We had to get up, it was time for chuck,
And also his morning grog.

Right after that we were under our hats
And the poodle beamed with pride.
He seemed to say, "Let's get on with the day,
Hey, boys, I'm ready to ride."

So we'd get saddled up and ready to track
And I'd put the dog up on his perch.
And with his claws in that sack, and his paws on Bob's back
The poodle would never lurch.

He'd stand there all day, 'cause for him it was play,
And he had no fear of a fall.
We crashed across rivers, spruce jungles, and swamps
And the poodle was having a ball.

What more could we ask, as in the sun he would bask,
There was horses and grub and grog.
And he felt no pain as we rode through the rain
This Apricot Poodle Dog.

He had his true friends, and sometimes he got gin,
And once he drank some Dram-boo,
But his favorite of all, as we rode through the fall,
Was an ice-cold glass of LaBatt's Blue.

He'd sit there and grin, as it ran down his chin,
And his whiskers were covered with foam.
And this little pink scamp, who rode like a champ,
Just loved his cowboy home.

We rode herd 'till fall, when we gathered them all,
Went home and got ready to ship.
And the Indians would grin at the crazy white men
And the horse with a dog on his hip.

Yeah, and the tourists would gape, like a big bunch of apes,
Whenever we got near,
'cause on the fly, we'd often stop by
And water at the Old Frontier.

Well, late in the fall when the wind commenced to squall
And we began to wean,
There was slop and rain and hail and sleet
And some cows turned damned mean.

And what happened then, I'll tell you friends,
It happened just like that.
An old wild cow, with a horny brow,
Had knocked the poodle flat.

He hit with a thud, right in the mud,
And I beat the cow off with my hat.
And Bob ran in and grabbed up our friend
And got him the hell out of that.

But we knew with a look, as the top hand shook,
That his riding days were through
And with a wee, little cough, he just seemed to slip off.
There was nothing that we could do.

Well, we thought all day about things we could say
And how to tell our wives.
What could we do about this canine true
Who had become such a part of our lives.

Well, we buried that dog with a bottle of grog,
He had worked for minimum wage,
And the feats will be told of this poodle bold
into another age.

So, with a howl and a hoot and a whiskey salute
We sent the poodle on his way.
And two cowboys cried around the fire that night
As we thought of a happier day.

After all these years, when friends draw near
And we speak of times gone by,
My bowlegged friend walks right on in—
He just refuses to die.

So whenever we gather to spin our tales
And remember days of old,
We toast our little pink friend, who rides in the wind,
The Apricot Poodle Bold.

## ABOUT THE EDITOR

*T*ed Stone has been traveling the Northern Range collecting stories and poems of the Canadian prairies, Montana, the Dakotas, and British Columbia for more than a decade. His best-selling books include The One That Got Away, Hailstorms and Hoop Snakes, *and* It's Hardly Worth Talkin' If You're Goin' To Tell The Truth. *Other work has been published in magazines and newspapers in both Canada and the United States. In addition to his writing, Stone regularly performs as a storyteller and speaker in schools, libraries, and before a variety of community and business groups across the Northern Range.*